COMMUNITY INTEGRATION
—— PLAYBOOK ——
A COMMUNITY-BASED SOLUTION
FOR WARRIOR EMPOWERMENT

America's Warrior Partnership
Jim Lorraine
President/CEO

Authored by the staff of
America's Warrior Partnership

America's Warrior Partnership's™ Playbook is a reflection of the collective
work and best practice methods used to implement the Four-Step Plan. It has
benefitted from the experiences of many direct service care providers.

Community Integration Playbook:
A Community-Based Solution for Warrior Empowerment ©
3rd Edition

America's Warrior Partnership
1190 Interstate Parkway
Augusta, Georgia 30909
706-434-1708
americaswarriorpartnership.org

America's Warrior Partnership would like to thank Jim Hull for the initiative to start this community veteran program and for his vision to seek to be a national model. His passion for this cause has fueled America's Warrior Partnership and empowered communities and warriors across the country.

America's Warrior Partnership would like to thank Wounded Warrior Project® for having the foresight to support our mission, which empowered us to publish this book.

ISBN 978-1-7324901-0-9

TABLE OF CONTENTS

PREFACE

by Jim Lorraine, President/CEO of America's Warrior Partnership

In 2005, when the United States Special Operations Command (USSOCOM) Care Coalition was founded, the majority of wounded, ill, or injured service members from our nation's global combat engagements were from within the special operations community. Servicemen and servicewomen from the US Army Special Operations Command, US Naval Special Warfare Command, US Air Force Special Operations Command, US Marines Corps Forces Special Operations Command, and the sub-unified Joint Special Operations Command are part of the special operations forces (SOF). These forces include Navy SEALs, Army Green Berets, Army Rangers, Army Special Operations Aviation Regiment, Air Force Air Commandos, and Marine Raiders.

Although special operations are functionally the best military forces in the world, in 2005 the USSOCOM was not equipped or authorized to provide the inpatient medical services and subsequent administrative management needed for care of the increasing numbers of wounded, ill, or injured service members. This situation presented a number of critical problems:

- Members of the USSOCOM felt like they were not keeping their promise to serve those who volunteer for difficult SOF jobs.
- Members of the SOF were losing confidence in the USSOCOM's commitment to care for them and their families.
- The SOF were losing capable and willing fighters to the administrative medical processes of the armed services.
- Both the USSOCOM and the wounded, ill, or injured were frustrated that no advocate existed to keep SOF and their families from slipping through the cracks.

The Care Coalition was founded to be the leader in connecting the needs of the SOF wounded, ill, or injured to the means of support available in the nation. Although USSOCOM did not have the resources or the authority to provide long-term support, it did have a relationship with the SOF wounded, ill, or injured that enabled the Care Coalition to educate and advocate for their long-term success. This trusting relationship with the forces, combined with the USSOCOM's ability to collaborate across government and nongovernmental service providers, empowered the Care Coalition to focus on the individual's goals while leveraging the services of existing programs to achieve the aims of the individual and the command.

To serve our forces, using the tenants of the SOF Truths[1] and USSOCOM's position as a national leader, I led the USSOCOM Care Coalition to take three steps:

> **SOF Truths**
> - Humans are more important than hardware.
> - Quality is better than quantity.
> - Special operations forces cannot be mass-produced.
> - Competent special operations forces cannot be created after emergencies occur.
> - Most special operations require non-SOF assistance.

1. Identify all SOF members wounded, ill, or injured during military service since September 11, 2001, regardless if still serving, separated, or retired, and develop a proactive relationship to understand their current place in life and where they wanted to go.

2. Simultaneously, build symbiotic relationships with government and nongovernmental programs that were currently supporting the wounded, ill, or injured while seeking out new programs that could enhance their quality of life.

3. Develop a process to track, manage, and measure the impact of our program to ensure we were empowering wounded, ill, or injured SOF members; their families; and the USSOCOM.

Since 2005, the USSOCOM Care Coalition built trusting relationships with thousands of wounded, ill, or injured SOF members. We provided them with the hope that no matter what the obstacle, they had an advocate by their side to ensure their success. We

---

[1]United States Special Operations Command, "SOF Truths," accessed March 3, 2018, http://www.socom.mil/about/sof-truths.

identified gaps and worked with hundreds of existing government and nongovernmental programs to fill those gaps. Moreover, we developed a program that used a relationship to add to a collective cultural change within the USSOCOM.

In the end, through proactive outreach and engagement with wounded, ill, or injured SOF members, the Care Coalition restored the SOF members' confidence in the USSOCOM. As a result, the USSOCOM developed confidence in the program and provided material support to ensure its success. Additionally, many gaps in service that had affected our wounded, ill, or injured in the past were closed, and hope for the future was opened. In my opinion, the most impactful outcomes were the derivatives of our human-centered approach that had not been considered when we started in 2005. These outcomes were as follows:

- Increased return-to-duty rate (retention)—In 2011, there were so many amputees operating in the combat zone that we considered placing a prosthetics lab in the combat zone.
- Increased recruitment/retention—As the Care Coalition's efforts to support and care for wounded, ill, or injured SOF members and their families became known, more service members were willing to join and stay in the SOF.
- A coalescing of service providers that collaborated toward each need—Through our measurement process, we could identify programs that we wanted to stick with and those that needed to improve. In the end, the number of partners became smaller, yet the partnerships had more impact.
- The reduction of the rate of suicide among wounded, ill, or injured SOF members—This decrease can be correlated to the depth of the trusted relationship that developed between the wounded, ill, or injured SOF members and the USSOCOM Care Coalition.
- Recognition outside the SOF community that "Humans are more important than hardware"—This recognition initiated from the SOF Truths and rippled out into the armed forces community at large.

The Beginning of Community Integration

In 2011, after leaving my position as the director of the USSOCOM Care Coalition, I became the executive director of a community veteran nonprofit in Augusta, Georgia. The group was raising awareness about the need for and ability of the community to serve active-duty wounded, ill, or injured and its community veterans. However, it did not take me long to realize that no one knew the veterans in the community. Most providers focused their work on those who were seeking services, and even then, there was little effort to coordinate the services among community nonprofits or government agencies.

Through the experience inspired by the Care Coalition's success, I believed it would be more effective for the community to first focus on the human aspect (veterans), then leverage the organizations. As a result, in 2012 the organization's aims shifted. Instead of trying to bring other organizations together, we focused on developing a relationship with community veterans and connected them to local organizations to provide the desired services. Reflecting the actions of the USSOCOM, we set out to complete three actions:

1. Identify all veterans living in the community, whether they needed support or not, by developing a proactive relationship and holistically understanding where they were in their lives and where they wanted to go.

2. Simultaneously, build symbiotic relationships with local government and nongovernmental programs that were serving our community in areas such as housing, education, employment, US Department of Veterans Affairs (VA) benefits, VA health care, recreation, spirituality, and personal relationships. At the same time, we sought new programs that could enhance veterans' quality of life.

3. Develop a process to track, manage, and measure the impact of our program to ensure we were empowering veterans, their families, and the community.

To accomplish this, we created a team to lead our outreach and engagement efforts to all veterans (Action 1) and another team to develop community partners to provide opportunities/solutions (Action 2). A four-step plan—connect, educate, advocate, and collaborate—was then developed to guide the teams' efforts.

1. **Connect** with community groups who could provide services and volunteer opportunities while also connecting with community veterans.

2. **Educate** the community about the value of veterans, and educate veterans about opportunities to improve their quality of life.

3. **Advocate** for the community (being the best in Georgia or the nation), and advocate for veterans and their families to navigate around obstacles that threaten to stop their process of improving their quality of life.

4. **Collaborate** with everyone who brings positive support to the community, veterans, and their families.

For more than a decade, I have personally witnessed how this four-step plan creates positive change and empowerment in the lives of military service members, veterans, and their families. America's Warrior Partnership invites you to join us in this mission. We look forward to working with you.

INTRODUCTION

AMERICA'S WARRIOR PARTNERSHIP

America's Warrior Partnership is a national nonprofit organization based in Augusta, Georgia. Our staff includes veterans, veteran and military family members, and civilians. Some of us have worked in community nonprofit human services for decades, whereas others have a business background or widely varied military operational specialties. Our board members are all volunteers and have diverse knowledge and experiences. Our team is united by the passionate belief that our nation can and must do better in supporting veterans and that the best way to serve veterans is by creating individual relationships within communities.

The mission of America's Warrior Partnership is to empower communities to empower veterans. We fill the gaps that exist between current veteran service organizations by helping nonprofits connect with veterans, military members, and families in need: bolstering their efficacy, improving their results, and empowering their initiatives. America's Warrior Partnership is a force multiplier for warrior Community Integration that enhances communities where great Americans choose to live and contribute. For more information on the organization and how to get involved, visit www.AmericasWarriorPartnership.org.

The Purpose of This Book

We believe communities are the best support for veterans, veterans deserve to be known and supported, and veterans make communities better places to live.

America's Warrior Partnership's Community Integration model is a warrior-focused model. This book is for any like-minded organizations that wish to use the Community Integration model to empower warriors in their community.

In this text, you will learn how to use this model in your community to know your veterans, rally existing resources, and improve the quality of life for veterans, their family members, caregivers, and survivors. We want to empower veterans, and we know the best way to do that is to empower every community in America to empower their hometown veterans.

Creation of Community Integration

In 2013, the Augusta Warrior Project was selected to implement a new program, Community Integration, funded by the Wounded Warrior Project®. The scope of this program necessitated the creation of a separate organization. America's Warrior Partnership was created to execute the Community Integration initiative.

The basis of Community Integration is the implementation of our four-step plan in communities across the nation, with the goal of ensuring that communities have the capacity to meet the needs of their warrior populations. Community Integration is designed to equip warrior-focused nonprofit organizations with the support necessary to carry out the **four-step plan** and to carry out a mission that will honor and empower warriors and their family members through sometimes-difficult transitions into and during civilian life.

The Community Integration initiative of America's Warrior Partnership believes that every community has a responsibility to serve "those who have borne the battle." America's Warrior Partnership wants to help every willing community **connect, educate, advocate,** and **collaborate** on behalf of warriors to establish an effective support system with the goal of successful reintegration into community life.

Definitions of Common Terms

As you read and use this *Playbook*, keep in mind that we geared the information to an audience with a medium amount of experience in nonprofit/human services.

Some topics may be a review for those who have more experience, whereas those new to the field can obtain additional resources from the America's Warrior Partnership support team. The following are frequently used terms in this *Playbook*:

Affiliate—An organization that has completed phases 1–3 of America's Warrior Partnership's Community Integration program, has demonstrated results based on the organization's stated goals, utilizes WarriorServe®, and has passed their Community Integration Comprehensive Audit.

Case coordination—An approach to human services characterized by attention to individual needs, advocacy to facilitate access to services and benefits, and effective resource management to promote quality service and positive outcomes.

Case coordinator or advocate—These terms are used interchangeably to mean a staff member who might be called a caseworker in other service organizations; a staff member who works directly with warriors to assist them in setting and reaching goals and solving their challenges.

Collaboration—Working cooperatively and deliberately with other professionals, organizations, or groups to achieve a goal.

Community Integration—Supporting and assisting warriors with transitions into and during civilian life.

Community Integration organization (CIO)—A nonprofit organization consulting with America's Warrior Partnership to implement the Community Integration model of warrior support.

Customer relationship management (CRM)—A CRM technology solution allows organizations to manage relationships, interactions, data, and information associated with warriors served.

Four-step plan—The foundation of Community Integration model: connect, educate, advocate, and collaborate with and for veterans and your community.

Holistic—Addressing many facets of a warrior's life as part of working with the warrior. America's Warrior Partnership identifies eight specific holistic life areas in our service model: housing, employment, education, access to earned benefits, recreation, physical and mental health, spirituality, and relationships.

Hot desk—In the Community Integration model, a hot desk is a physical space at a partner's location to meet with warriors and be available for outreach, engagement, or case coordination and to communicate/collaborate with the partner's staff.

Toolkit—An electronic folder of resources available to organizations following America's Warrior Partnership's Community Integration model. The Toolkit contains examples of forms and more information about specific concepts identified in this Playbook.

Warrior—A military veteran or a military service member. We support warriors and their family members or caregivers. Any use of the term *warrior* in this book is meant to include veterans, service members, their family members, caregivers, and survivors.

WarriorServe®—America's Warrior Partnership's CRM tool developed in support of the Community Integration model. This tool is a warrior-centric, cost-effective, and secure information system that streamlines the collection of warrior data and provides a closed-loop follow-up to ensure no case is left unresolved.

CHAPTER 1:
COMMUNITY INTEGRATION

What's in this chapter?

✓ The context for the necessity of Community Integration
✓ A description of Community Integration
✓ The main principles of Community Integration

"Any nation which does not honor its heroes will not long endure."

~ Abraham Lincoln,
Sixteenth President of the United States

WHY COMMUNITY INTEGRATION?

The Charge

All communities have a responsibility to their sons and daughters who voluntarily served our nation to protect our Constitution and way of life. That responsibility includes finding them and helping them understand their veteran benefits and also helping them to reintegrate into their communities.

The Problem

According to data from the US Department of Veteran Affairs, US Census Bureau, and noted experts, there are currently approximately 18,600,000[2] veterans with at least 26,000,000[3] immediate family members living in the United States. Almost 50 percent of all veterans are unknown or unassisted by national and state government programs. Additionally, without accounting for membership in multiple groups, approximately six million are members served by the national veteran service organizations. This gap of roughly nine million veterans and thirteen million family members is both an opportunity to serve and a challenge to strengthen our nation. America's Warrior Partnership's experience has verified that this national ratio of known veterans to unknown veterans is carried to the state and community level either because communities are not acknowledging the service of our veterans or because the veterans do not identify themselves as veterans.

Some of the nine million veterans not accessing government or nongovernmental services may not have a need because they transitioned to civilian life well or may not yet need to utilize the services that they have earned. However, it is unknown how many of these millions are living in the shadows due to lack of awareness, initiative, or ability. We will never know unless we engage the broad demographic of veterans and assess their reason for lack of engagement.

[2]National Center for Veterans Analysis and Statistics, "Profile of Veterans: 2016," last modified 2016, https://www.va.gov/vetdata/docs/SpecialReports/Profile_of_Veterans_2016.pdf.

[3]D. Segal, R. Blum, G. Gorman, and V. Maholmes, The Effects of Military Deployment on Family Health (Washington, DC: National Press Club, 2001), http://www.prb.org/pdf11/segal-military-families-presentation.pdf.

The Call of Duty

We have heard many reasons why it is unimaginable to "know" all our nation's veterans. The naysayers declare, "There are too many—it will take too long"; "They do not want to be known"; "They are not eligible"; "If they need something, they will ask." However, these voices do not know for sure; no one does.

What we do know is the following:

- Until communities build relationships with their veterans, they will never understand the veterans living in their communities.
- The time to start is now, and the place to start is at the community level that expands outwardly to a national effort.
- There are far more veterans who are eligible for earned services and not seeking them than there are veterans who are ineligible.

Consider this experience of America's Warrior Partnership.

A local education partner noted that out of four thousand students attending the university, only fifty-eight veterans registered were utilizing their GI Bill benefits. Knowing there were more than fifty-eight veterans among the four thousand students, we did an in-depth outreach campaign to identify all the veterans attending college. Within ninety days, the school had identified over 215 student veterans. Sadly, half of the newly identified students were eligible for the post-9/11 GI Bill but did not use it because when they left the service, the bill had not been enacted, and no one communicated its availability. These students had taken loans, worked second jobs, and struggled to pay for school because no one asked them if they had served in the military or discussed their opportunities.

There are many of these cases, not just with younger veterans but also with older veterans who should have filed a benefits claim and never did because they "got on with their lives." For some of these older veterans, a claim is the deciding factor between staying in their homes or going to an assisted-living environment. As expert veteran service connectors, we all know someone whom we wished that we had met six months earlier so that we could have helped prevent a greater crisis.

The Scope of Need and Opportunity

- Approximately 18,600,000 veterans are living in the United States.

- Across the United States, 3,142 counties are home to an average of 6,679 veterans per county.

- There is an estimated total of forty to forty-five thousand veteran-serving nongovernmental organizations throughout the nation, existing to serve veterans and their families, caregivers, and survivors.

- There are 152 US Department of Veterans Affairs (VA) medical centers in the United States and 150 military installations located in communities throughout the country.

The opportunity exists at the community level to collectively lead outreach efforts to veterans by following America's Warrior Partnership's four-step model of **connect, educate, advocate**, and **collaborate**.

THE SOLUTION

"1. Everyone wants to succeed. 2. Success is contagious."
—Bob McDonald,
Former U.S. Secretary of Veteran Affairs

Initiating a formal Community Integration program focused on building a relationship with warriors to understand their life goals and then connecting warriors with existing government and nongovernmental services within the community will not only improve the quality of life for the warriors and their families but also improve the quality of life for the community.

Additionally, veterans who are currently not in need of services are often seeking purpose in life. Many find that volunteerism provides that purpose by allowing them to give back and be a part of something larger than themselves. All too often, they are the community leaders who never spoke of their service or successful businesspeople wanting to give back but not sure how.

Our ultimate challenge and opportunity to serve and give back to our warriors can be found in the nine million unknown veterans. It is these veterans, the unknown among those who have served our nation in uniform, that, through their connection with services and their empowerment, will strengthen the fabric of our local communities.

Through America's Warrior Partnership's Community Integration model, we empower communities to empower warriors.

The following are best practices for communities to empower warriors:

- All warriors should be known.
- Warriors and their families are the sole focus. Treat each warrior individually and holistically.
- Create and use a process that is both respectful of warriors and effective.
- Act as a clearinghouse to coordinate services and provide partner accountability.
- Maintain an advocate relationship with warriors until they achieve their personal goals.

The solution demands proactive outreach and engagement utilizing America's Warrior Partnership's holistic four-step model.

"The willingness with which our young people are likely to serve in any war, no matter how justified, shall be directly proportional to how they perceive veterans of earlier wars were treated and appreciated by our nation."
—George Washington

WHAT IS COMMUNITY INTEGRATION?

At the foundation of America's Warrior Partnership's model is the belief that no one who has served our country during any era, in any branch of military service, should ever be in need of housing, employment, training, or health benefits or want for a purposeful endeavor. This model embraces a holistic approach to warrior care that relies on case coordination and advocacy, rather than on simple problem solving. It is a solution-focused model, starting with a solution and then empowering warriors and their family members to develop a plan that will lead to that solution.

 Provides Support for All Warriors

The warriors in your community come from a variety of social, economic, employment, and personal backgrounds. Warriors who are already community leaders bring a different set of circumstances to the table than homeless Warriors, and a different amount of effort is required to support each of those people as they pursue success and well-being as they individually define it. All individuals can be mapped on a continuum of their need for assistance and their means or resources to assist themselves.

The following diagram illustrates a general rule of thumb for the potential improvement in the community's quality of life to be gained by investing effort to increase the means and decrease the needs of warriors.

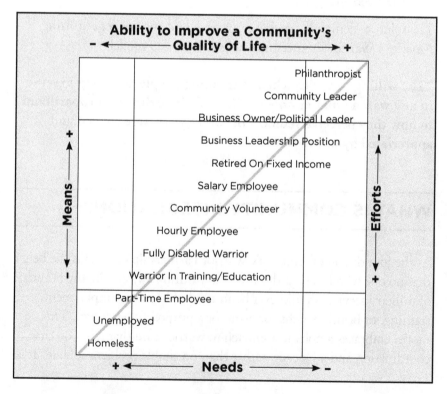

Ability to Improve a Community's Quality of Life:
- Through community service/leadership
- For warriors, family, friends, and community
- In terms of contribution of time, talent, and treasure

Efforts:
- The amount of organizational effort it takes to address a need or continue engagement
- The amount of effort to find and engage the warrior

Needs:
- Include housing, education, employment, benefits, health care, advocacy, and behavioral health

Means:
- Include financial, emotional, motivational, intellectual, advocacy, network of supporters, and spiritual/family support

The homeless warrior has many **needs** but little **means**. It takes a community organization a lot of **effort** to assist the homeless warrior at a time when this warrior has little ability to improve the **quality of life** of the community. The inverse is true for the philanthropist.

By serving warriors who come from different backgrounds, you increase the likelihood that greater returns will come to the community from each warrior's success. You also increase the likelihood that you will assist more warriors and help each of them have a chance to pursue their own solutions. Focusing all your efforts on warriors who have low means and high need might use up all your community's resources so that no time is left to work with warriors who have middle or high means and lower need. And focusing only on warriors who have little need or sufficient means might cause your community to miss the opportunity to make huge changes in the lives of warriors who struggle greatly and cannot change their lives without help.

 A Solution-Focused Approach

A solution-focused approach to warrior care does the following:

1. Accepts a person in his or her current situation
2. Identifies his or her strengths and resources
3. Builds on actions the person is already doing
4. Utilizes a plan with achievable steps
5. Remains oriented toward a solution, rather than a problem
6. Moves toward a goal of how the person wishes to see the future

It is a personalized, "one-size-fits-one" approach. It is meant to not only help a warrior solve a current problem but also encourage the warrior to learn strategies to successfully and independently address future challenges in new and constructive ways.

 Warrior Case-Coordination Model

The premise of America's Warrior Partnership's model is that resources already exist for warrior care in every community. All warriors in need can be reached by collaborating with existing resource providers, focusing on warriors, and working in concert with the community to fill gaps in services. This model places a heavy reliance on community collaboration in which warrior consumers are referred to other organizations for direct services, and the lead warrior service organization accepts warrior consumer referrals from other organizations. Such an approach eliminates duplication of services and strengthens the whole community's groups. This collaboration requires the building of bridges between the military culture and the community at large.

 Requires a Lead Organization
for Veteran Case Coordination

America's Warrior Partnership's model aims to designate one agency within the community as the lead for warrior outreach and coordination, regardless of which agency provides the direct services. The lead organization must complete a comprehensive, holistic assessment of each warrior. This assessment must go beyond merely solving the presenting problem, such as homelessness. It also requires leadership in the community. The goal for every warrior is empowerment in all areas of life and a feeling of well-being; this can be accomplished only with purposeful coordination of community resources and active collaboration.

The work of an organization using America's Warrior Partnership's model should always create solutions for warriors through strengths-based assessments and client-centered case coordination, applied in a community (systems) framework.[4] If followed, this model will result in a comprehensive community network of resources, holistic care for warriors, and real solutions.

Introduction to the Eleven Principles of Community Integration

1. Serve all warriors

Veteran-focused organizations following the Community Integration model will serve all warriors and their family members or caregivers from any era and any character of discharge. Serving and creating a trusting relationship with this diverse population of warriors means knowing the struggling and the successful, the young and the old, the employee and the employer, the teacher and the student. This diversity empowers those veterans with the ability to provide a hand to those who are struggling. Through these trusting relationships, veterans seek assistance before the crisis occurs, they seek advice on volunteer opportunities and ways to give back, and they spread the word and become part of something larger than themselves.

2. You can only serve warriors you know

Proactive outreach is the most important aspect of Community Integration. Proactive outreach refers to the actual face-to-face encounter with a warrior, with the express intent to develop a relationship with recurring interactions. Proactive outreach should take you into the community to find warriors. Extensive, proactive outreach

---

[4] Lee Flamand, "Systems Theory of Social Work," Synonym, last modified October 4, 2017, http://classroom.synonym.com/systems-theory-of-social-work-12079509.html.

efforts are the foundation of an organization's Community Integration program.

3. You can only know warriors if you connect with them

Engagement meets warriors in their current personal situations, working or unemployed, well or ill, stably housed or homeless, financially well off or declaring bankruptcy. Engagement means assessing the full spectrum of potential need and that the warrior is actively involved in creating the plan to address areas of growth or activity. Community Integration focuses on building strong relationships through individual connections with warriors and service providers and by the coordination of available community resources.

4. A holistic approach increases warrior success

A holistic approach addresses all areas of total warrior care and fulfillment and ensures that no one need is singled out. In this holistic approach, the concentrated areas are housing, employment, education, benefits, health care, and wellness supported through recreation, relationships, spiritual health and mental health.

5. One size fits one warrior

Every warrior is different in terms of life situation, life factors, and dreams. Case coordination for warriors is not a cookie-cutter process. It is as unique as each individual warrior.

6. Work with warriors is sustained and sequential

Work with warriors is planned and deliberate. Addressing the initial need of a warrior includes learning what the warrior wants his or her life to look like in five years and making sure the warrior's holistic care plan sets incremental, measurable, and meaningful goals to build toward the ultimate success. Your organization is committing to work with each warrior until he or she reaches his or her long-term objectives and then to maintain a relationship beyond the completion of these objectives.

7. The four-step plan increases community success

To facilitate a solution-focused model, America's Warrior Partnership has developed and implemented a four-step plan to promote the linking of warriors to community resources. Our four-step plan (connect, educate, advocate, and collaborate) is designed to successfully implement America's Warrior Partnership's model within your community. This solution-focused model, with an emphasis on case coordination, stresses engagement with warriors and family members, meeting them where they live, on their terms, and within already functioning educational, vocational, and social systems. The plan catalyzes resources to assist warriors in obtaining existing services and overcoming barriers that may impede their successful adaptation to civilian life.

8. Community Integration leaders are authentic, transparent, and pursue excellence

Community Integration organizations establish themselves as leaders in their communities by doing the following:
- Being trusted and transparent
- Doing what's right
- Providing high-quality and complete services
- Embracing best practices
- Undertaking current and future innovation

9. Resources for warriors already exist in each community

There are up to forty-five thousand veteran-serving nonprofits in the United States, not including government programs, that provide resources for veterans and their families. Additionally, veterans can receive support from human service resources that exist in every community for the general population. As a result, most veteran issues can be addressed locally with maximum collaboration.

10. Duplication of efforts wastes community resources

A notable distinction exists between duplication and replication of services. Duplication occurs when an organization sets out to offer something that already is provided in the same area to the same constituency. Duplication of services is almost always a poor social services practice. There may be times when it is appropriate to replicate a service offered by another agency because the service is needed in another location or desired by another group of consumers or because that agency is not in a position to expand the services it offers. Replication that is done to meet existing community needs with the cooperation or blessing of the original service provider is good for the community.

11. If you do the work, the funding will come

Our cyclic model is to start with just enough staff, who can work with a small number of veterans at a time. Prove your efforts, make a difference, and achieve results. Then, tell the community about your results so that the community will continue to support your organization and you can grow and do more work.

CHAPTER 2:
HOW DO YOU USE
THE FOUR-STEP PLAN?

What's in this chapter?

✓ A detailed explanation of America's Warrior Partnership's four-step plan
✓ Concrete examples of how each step can be used to support the principles of Community Integration

"The best way to promote and protect opportunities is through collaboration, consensus-building, and pragmatic problem-solving. Throughout nearly 30 years in public service, I have approached tough challenges by making room for as many people as possible around the table in search of common ground."

~ Thomas E. Perez,
Former U.S. Secretary of Labor

THE FOUR-STEP PLAN

America's Warrior Partnership's four-step plan (connect, educate, advocate, and collaborate) is designed to assist your organization in the successful implementation of Community Integration within your community.

There are two facets to each step of the four-step plan. One focuses on the warrior, and the other focuses on the community.

CONNECT

Build a relationship with all warriors in the community.

Build a relationship with service providers in the community.

EDUCATE

Inform warriors of services and opportunities available to them.

Inform and educate the community about the value of warriors and how to best support them.

ADVOCATE

Advocate, ensuring warriors receive the support they earned.

Advocate for the community to ensure appropriate services exist that will strengthen support for warriors.

COLLABORATE

Work with the veteran to create a holistic plan to improve the veteran's life.

Work with existing community providers to support warriors.

Work with partners outside the community to bring resources to the community.

Work with partners on all levels to facilitate total warrior care.

Utilizing the four-step plan as the framework for Community Integration requires planning, knowledge of available resources, a robust network of collaborating partners, and a means to measure and capture outcomes. In our experience, communities can address 90 percent of warriors' needs from within the community. By working with other communities, states, and national partners, communities can close the gap in their capacity to support the other 10 percent of warriors' needs.

America's Warrior Partnership will support and work with each community to personalize the implementation of the four-step plan to ensure you successfully meet your organization's program goals and objectives. Additionally, the *Playbook* Toolkit contains specific examples and detailed information to aid your organization in its execution of the four-step plan.

Connect

Connect includes both building a relationship with warriors and establishing a trusted relationship with other community service providers. Connect is the first step in the four-step plan because it is the foundation upon which all other steps are built. To succeed, you must first create personal connections to warriors and join with other community service organizations that can assist your efforts to empower warriors.

The following are recommendations for and examples of ways to **connect** with warriors and the community:

- Establish a community organization to be the single point of contact to build a relationship with all warriors seeking assistance or personal growth opportunities.
- Network and build working relationships with community organizations to holistically address warriors' interests.
- Identify and connect with all warriors through a proactive, comprehensive outreach program.
- Orchestrate and participate in local events that are relevant to all warriors so that the lead community organization can establish relationships.
- Implement a customer relationship management (CRM) tool that allows the lead veteran-centric organization the ability to electronically refer cases to partners and vice versa and allows

warriors to identify themselves to the lead veteran community organization; veteran-serving organizations are able to support warriors by connecting them to the resources they need.

- Develop processes to holistically assess warriors and connect them to community partners that can address their identified needs.
- Involve warriors in the planning and implementation of their holistic personal goals and objectives from assessment through achievement or completion.
- Develop relationships and identify shared goals with community partners.
- Engage stakeholders in the community in the development of a comprehensive approach that will ensure best practices.

Educate

After you have begun connecting with warriors and other community service organizations, it is time to take the next step and begin educating warriors about the community services available to them. Additionally, your organization must commence educating the community about the value the veteran population brings to your community. The program impact evaluation done within the Community Analysis, which can be created for you by America's Warrior Partnership, contains a valuable chart, America's Warrior Partnership's Index of Veteran Economic Impact (on a community), detailing the economic benefits veterans bring to your community.

The following are recommendations and examples of ways to **educate** warriors and the community:

- Educate the community as a whole about the needs of warriors and their value to the community.
- Inform warriors of the opportunities and services available to them both locally and nationally, including benefits earned via their military service.
- Advise community leadership to engage agencies in addressing problems and providing solutions (e.g., partnerships, roundtable meetings).

- Develop and implement an operational plan for your organization that reduces red tape, eliminates duplication of efforts, and effectively focuses on results for both warriors and the community.
- Develop and maintain a community resource directory, which can be created for you by America's Warrior Partnership, called the Community Profile Map. This map identifies resources, contacts, and other relevant information. This directory should include information such as contacts at local organizations that provide direct services, national groups with available funding or services for which your local warriors may qualify, and the eligibility requirements to access them.

Advocate

Advocacy includes both speaking up in support of warrior concerns and taking specific actions on behalf of individual warriors. Advocacy actions occur when a warrior needs assistance to overcome an obstacle encountered in the warrior's holistic care plan. The advocate's job is to ensure the obstacle is blocking a legitimate need and teach the warrior, through the advocacy process, how to address similar impediments independently in the future. Advocacy on a community level involves providing information on specific veteran issues within the community to move the public to action and serving as a liaison between the veteran community and public and government agencies.

The following are recommendations for and examples of ways to **advocate** for warriors and the community:

- Utilize a solution-focused case-coordination approach for warriors.
- Navigate through the complex resources, benefits, and opportunities available to warriors.
- Advocate for greater awareness in the community for warriors.
- Establish a high standard of warrior care locally through a well-developed model and well-executed plan.
- Ensure warriors and their families receive the support they have earned.
- Ensure community resources are developed and sustained to improve the warrior's quality of life.

Collaborate

Collaboration is the last step in the four-step plan. By connecting, educating, and advocating, you have placed your organization on the radar as the go-to organization for warriors. However, it is the last step, collaboration, that will assist your efforts in becoming the leader for warrior care in your community. Through collaboration, you build bridges within your community to ensure your organization is involved in identifying, addressing, and creating solutions for issues germane to warriors.

The following are recommendations for and examples of ways to **collaborate** with warriors and the community:

- Establish trusted relationships in the community.
- Seek opportunities for greater educational, employment, housing, social, recreational, and wellness opportunities for warriors.
- Be a leader in information flow, and encourage ideas with partners and stakeholders.
- Work effectively with warriors to provide them holistic care.
- Work effectively with partners and stakeholders at all levels to facilitate total warrior service.
- Enhance the resources available in the community for warriors. Create solutions to fill gaps in the services provided to warriors.
- Bridge the gap between warriors and life-changing resources by providing access to state, federal, and local education benefits; local employment opportunities; housing; job training; college resources; health care; and other community services.
- Embrace relationships, networks of partners, and a system of shared goals with partner organizations.
- Set an example by modeling best practices in warrior service and organization operations, and encourage other agencies to follow best practices.

CHAPTER HIGHLIGHTS

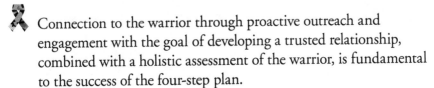 Connection to the warrior through proactive outreach and engagement with the goal of developing a trusted relationship, combined with a holistic assessment of the warrior, is fundamental to the success of the four-step plan.

To succeed, you must first create personal connections with warriors and join with other community service organizations that can assist your efforts to empower warriors.

Education, advocacy, and collaboration with and for the warrior and the community are the building blocks that improve quality of life for our warriors, their families, caregivers, and survivors and develop a stronger community.

CHAPTER 3:
PUTTING COMMUNITY INTEGRATION INTO ACTION

What's in this chapter?

✓ How to initiate Community Integration
  in your community

✓ Tips and strategies for the following:
  - Finding warriors
  - Knowing warriors
  - Serving warriors
    – Suggestions for holistic warrior support
    – Specifics about becoming the leader
    – Best practices for collaboration

"The secret of getting ahead is getting started."

- Mark Twain

FINDING THE WARRIOR

The base of the four-step plan, and the most crucial step, is **connect**. It is this actual face-to-face encounter with a warrior, with the express intent to develop a relationship with recurring interactions, that is foundational to your organization's success. Merely having a veteran program will not ensure success in your community. Outreach is not sitting at your desk and hoping warriors will walk into your office. You must go into the community and actively seek out and engage those you wish to serve.

Warrior Outreach: The Direct Method for Warrior Engagement

The first encounter with a veteran is critical because this meeting establishes the veteran's willingness to connect with your organization.

The objectives of this meeting are as follows:
1. To build rapport
2. To obtain necessary information so that you can contact the warrior for further details at a more appropriate time

> **TIPS** ✪ Initiate a conversation as you would with anyone you are interested in knowing.
> ✪ Don't worry about getting all the information that you need for your documentation. If you are too focused on filling out a form, you might miss out on vital information that the person is offering.
> ✪ If you are at an event, keep your conversations short. Your goal is to connect with many warriors, family members, and caregivers; not just one.

A key strategy for proactive outreach is identifying where your target warriors would go—where they work, live, worship, and play.

Think strategically about your target warriors:
- What era are they from?
- What hobbies might they have?
- Be careful not to limit yourself to only engaging with veterans in designated outreach events.

- Visit many places; attend different events. Outreach possibilities occur everywhere (e.g., at the gym, the grocery store, or a kid's soccer game).

EXAMPLE | A restaurant that is typically patronized by people over the age of sixty would not likely be a place to engage post-9/11 warriors, but it might be an excellent place to find retired pre-9/11 warriors.

If you live near a military installation and have a veteran staff member, explore opportunities to connect with the transition services. Attending the transition meetings can help you extend outreach efforts to veterans who intend to transition into your community. Developing this relationship can take time, and it can be difficult to establish initially.

Community Engagement: The Indirect Method of Outreach

Community engagement is integral to leveraging the wide-ranging support that is necessary to provide well-rounded, actionable solutions for veterans.

Proactive community-outreach and relationship-maintenance efforts will directly impact your community engagement by
- connecting warriors to services in your community,
- educating your community on the importance of the services provided,
- helping your organization to develop partnerships and collaborative services, and
- increasing your organization's ability to receive sustainable community support and funding.

Who Is Responsible for Community Outreach?

Community outreach is continuous work that requires effort by every team member. Outreach starts at the top and extends down to everyone in your organization, from your board members to your volunteers.

- All team members, volunteers, board members, and community partners should understand your mission because everyone will be an ambassador for the organization.

✪ It is a good idea to develop a fact sheet that lists your organization's services and impact, to be handed out at community events, fairs, and speaking engagements.

✪ To assist staff and volunteers, consider creating a research sheet that includes information about the organization to which they are speaking. Make sure this information includes what the group has done in the past for warriors and their families, and a few ideas about what they can do to help your organization today—if the audience is motivated, a suggestion about how they can assist might turn into an immediate donation of time, talent, or treasure.

What Are Some Ways to Conduct Community Outreach?

1. Speak at group meetings or community events.
   - Tailor your message to your audience.
     - If you are speaking to a family readiness group, you do not have to educate them on the issues warriors are facing; they are well aware. Instead, you may want to speak about the need for volunteers and outreach to connect with those in need of services.
     - If you are speaking to the members of the local chamber of commerce, you may want to educate them on the number of warriors in their municipality, the valuable assets warriors can become with strong community support, and the skill sets they bring to the table.

2. Utilize media outlets to keep the community and followers informed of your organization's significant achievements and pending events. (See the Development and Marketing section in the Toolkit for specific marketing strategies.)
   - Develop partnerships with the local media.
   - Create social media blasts.
   - Post information about events and successes on your organization's website.
   - Create a newsletter.

3. Seek to work with other community service organizations and veteran service providers. Support their missions by
   - partnering with them to assist their veterans while seeking their expertise to serve the warriors and families at your organization, and
   - participating in their events that may attract warriors and their family members—this will not only assist your organization in its outreach efforts but will also help engage and educate the community as well.

Community outreach is part of building your organization's reputation as the "go-to" place for warrior issues. The result of being seen and being engaged in the community is that your organization will become a recognized veteran-support leader in the community.

KNOWING THE WARRIOR

At the beginning of the process, assessment and engagement establish the foundation of the relationship between your organization and the warrior. Your organization is to position itself to be a lifetime resource for your veterans; developing a relationship or providing a service is not a "one-and-done" action. Your staff conducting the intake should engage the warrior and gather information about his or her strengths, resources, and needs. This information will provide the basis for the warrior's holistic plan and goal setting.

> **TIPS** Although it is always best to meet the veteran in person, be sure to check your organization's policy for home visits before visiting homebound warriors.
>
> If your organization does not have a policy, consider the following suggestions:
> ✪ Never go alone; always take a colleague.
> ✪ Arrange to meet the warrior at the US Department of Veterans Affairs (VA) office when he or she goes for a scheduled appointment.
> ✪ Consider technology solutions that offer face-to-face interactions.

> ✪ If the veteran has VA home-based primary care services in place, consider coordinating home visits with the care team.

The Intake Assessment

We only know what we know, so it is vital to complete a comprehensive intake assessment with each warrior you hope to serve.

> **TIP** Use an intake form and a standard procedure to assist in the gathering of this information (see the Toolkit for a sample intake form). This process will also assist in the determination of eligibility for services and the level or type of services provided to the warrior. Consider using an electronic intake method, like the one found in WarriorServe®, to help reduce duplication of efforts.

Some important concepts to keep in mind as you complete the intake process are as follows:

 Accuracy and completeness—Collecting all needed data, as well as correct data, has the following benefits:
- Supports effective work and reporting
- Ensures that work does not need to be repeated to make corrections or additions

 Assessment—A proper intake process will help make initial determinations about eligibility for services offered by organizations and the level or type of services needed by the warrior. The following considerations apply to the assessment process:
- Be mindful that personal opinions and values may influence how you interpret the warrior's information.
- It is essential to be able to look at the warrior's situation from the warrior's perspective.
- Ask questions to ensure that you understand what the warrior is seeking and to reassure the warrior that you comprehend his or her situation.

Setting a tone—Creating a welcoming, trusting relationship between a warrior and an advocate sets the stage for a working relationship that will support the warrior in achieving her or his goals. It is vital for your organization to develop trusting relationships to
  • successfully assist warriors over the course of their lives, and
  • be seen as leaders in your local veteran space.

Listening—Using the following listening techniques will ensure that both you and the warrior are engaging in the conversation and in the task of forming the warrior's holistic plan:
  • Active listening
    – Give your undivided attention to the conversation. Remove all distractions and turn off your cell phone. Do not have side conversations with other people or leave to have another "quick" meeting.
    – Show your participation with verbal and nonverbal cues.
    – Refrain from interrupting the warrior or finishing thoughts/ sentences for him or her.
  • Reflective listening
    – Listen so that you can restate what the warrior has told you in your own words.
    – Confirm that what you have heard is what the warrior intended to express.

The goals that warriors set are their goals; you will only learn what is critical to warriors by listening to them.

Communication and teamwork—If the warrior needs assistance when you are not available or begins working with another staff member, the warrior should not have to repeat information included in the intake and assessment process. Effective communication involves the following:
  • Promptly entering complete information into your customer relationship management (CRM) tracking system/database— This allows other team members to know what you know about a warrior.

- All team members reading the information gathered at intake (and later)—This shared knowledge will help thwart any attempts a warrior may make to play team members against each other or get a different answer from a different person.

> **TIP** When referring a veteran to another advocate on your team or in the community, be sure that the veteran is informed about who the new advocate is and what service the advocate will be providing. If you are able, a quick introduction is always appreciated.

The Warrior's Holistic Plan

The goals identified during the assessment are prioritized and incorporated into the warrior's holistic plan, which is developed in conjunction with the warrior and, in some cases, family members. (An example of a warrior's holistic plan can be found in the Toolkit.)

The development of this holistic plan provides the warrior and advocates a step-by-step approach to goal attainment. This holistic plan includes the following elements:
- A short summary of the warrior's intake information
- Short- and long-term goals
- Actions for achieving the goals that are divided into manageable tasks
- Identification of the person responsible for the completion of each task
- Proposed task-completion dates
- Plans for follow-up

Supporting Documents

The supporting documents required in each warrior's file will vary from program to program and depend on the warrior's needs and holistic plan.

At a minimum, all case files should include the following elements:
1. A copy of the warrior's DD214 form when applicable
2. The intake form

3. The release of personal information (consumer authorization) form signed by the warrior, which will allow the base level of information release required for your organization's case-coordination/CRM tracking software and your reporting requirements (See the Toolkit for a sample consumer authorization form.)

Your organization may have other requirements related to privacy of personal information for the warriors you serve. More information is available under the "Ethics and Confidentiality in Service" heading in chapter 8.

Building Trust

Once a veteran is known, it is important to build trust. It is best for a community organization to manage expectations, deliver on what it promises, and not overpromise. This trust is built one step at a time but must be sustained through regular communications and being true to your word.

SERVING THE WARRIOR

Building a Support Network

We believe Community Integration has ignited a cultural shift and transformation in the way in which military veterans and their families reacclimate to civilian life. It starts with organizations like yours, complementing and leveraging government services, reinforced by civically engaged neighbors interested in embracing veterans because they know that veterans make their community stronger. Through community building, organizations serving veterans can gain an honest assessment of the gaps, challenges, and trends military veterans and their families are facing.

We believe no single agency can solve every pressing issue, but by utilizing our four-step plan, leading agencies can coalesce a purposeful network of organizations and individuals who serve veterans in need as well as those who are thriving. These efforts help us learn how capable a community is at prioritizing veterans' needs and demonstrating the value they bring. By elevating the veteran community, we end up uplifting the community as a whole and making it better for everyone.

> **TIP** Communicating with warriors through regular, focused, and relevant contact is more important than providing services. Through our annual surveys, America's Warrior Partnership has learned that veterans feel a greater sense of well-being from the community when they are communicated with every couple of weeks. The positive sense of well-being diminishes the less frequently they are contacted. Just as a business must communicate with its customers to maintain their loyalty, so must a community nonprofit that builds a relationship with all veterans.

America's Warrior Partnership provides the following services to assist you in the creation of a warrior support network:

- Performs initial research that illustrates a picture of the overall distribution of veterans within your community
- Develops a Community Analysis that assists your organization's plans to address warriors holistically within your community
- Creates a Community Profile Map that allows you to view resources available in the community that support the holistic approach
- Assists you in your implementation of America's Warrior Partnership Community Integration, a program that provides holistic care and addresses the person's entire situation, not just the presenting problem

Serve Veterans Holistically through Collaborative Service

America's Warrior Partnership Community Integration philosophy reinforces eight areas that are integral to a warrior's quality of life.

By addressing veterans holistically, issues are linked and identified early, crises are averted, and balance is created. When providing holistic support, the following areas must be addressed:

1. **Permanent housing**
2. **Meaningful employment**
3. **Strong family/friend relationships**

4. **Spirituality**
5. **Education and training**
6. **Access to earned benefits**
7. **Physical, mental, and behavioral health**
8. **Pursuit of recreation**

- The eight areas of America's Warrior Partnership's philosophy are all-encompassing. You will see overlap and might identify subcategories of needs.

- Correctly identifying core partnerships that can provide solutions for critical needs, wants, and desires will enhance the veteran's quality of life. These eight areas of holistic support work hand in hand. If one of these aspects of a veteran's life is incomplete or unfulfilled, that individual can be out of balance. (For additional criteria for partner selection, see "Tips for Selecting WarriorServe® Partner Portal Users" in the Toolkit.)

- Diversify your known veteran population to understand your veterans better and recognize gaps in your community. Identify and fill gaps in remote or underserved areas, but also target areas with a high prevalence of veteran success as well.

- Your organization should educate health-care providers, shelters, veteran service organizations (VSOs), and nonprofits to recognize and understand warrior issues and resources. You want to ensure the warrior community has a sound support network while simultaneously providing wraparound case-coordination services.

- America's Warrior Partnership's annual survey has documented that in addition to the eight areas of holistic support, quality of life is dependent on a sense of hope and purpose. A warrior's sense of connection to the community increases as engagement with a Community Integration organization increases, and a sense of well-being increases after a trusted relationship is established with a Community Integration organization.

America's Warrior Partnership's model emphasizes regularly measuring an individual's quality of life throughout the life cycle of interaction. By proactively monitoring veterans' well-being, Community Integration organizations are able to catch signs of hopelessness early.

What Should Holistic Warrior Support Look Like in My Organization?

• Permanent Housing

Providing housing to warriors and their family members can also indirectly impact education, employment, and reduction of mental health challenges. Having stable, dignified, and affordable housing, especially when coupled with low barriers to receiving resources, allows warriors and family members to focus on recovery and reintegration challenges and confront conditions that contribute to homelessness.

The following are the primary organization expectations necessary to provide housing support to veterans seeking permanent housing:

- Understand what services and grants are provided by your local VA office, including the Department of Housing and Urban Development–Veterans Affairs Supportive Housing (HUD-VASH) program, and stay up to date on eligibility requirements to ensure you make educated referrals.

- Work with local shelters and Stand Down events.
- Build relationships with organizations that provide services through the trajectory of housing/homelessness initiatives.
- Become an active part of your local continuum of care for the homeless, and encourage the whole community to tackle the issue of homelessness and the lack of safe, affordable housing.
- Network with community members as well as VA program leads to ensure community-wide marketing of programs.
- Connect warriors seeking housing assistance to available community resources.

How you offer housing services can vary greatly, from linking warriors and family members to existing emergency shelters and transitional, supportive, and independent housing programs to providing supportive services that contribute to self-sufficiency.

To meet your organization's housing objectives, it is imperative that your organization employ the following strategies:

- Identify all local nonprofits and community providers that offer housing assistance, and develop relationships/partnerships with them. Determine if your community is a recipient of any VA grant

---

TIPS ✪ Reach out to local banks for programming ideas; they often offer free community classes dealing with budgeting, savings, retirement, credit, and a variety of other financial issues. They can assist you in developing a program that will address the specific needs of your local veteran population.

✪ Often you will find several local organizations (private and nonprofit) that can assist with emergency financial or housing issues (e.g., Veterans of Foreign Wars [VFW], American Legion, social services). However, be sure to research and use national organizations as well.

✪ Provide, or ensure another warrior advocate is providing, a comprehensive service plan to all warriors receiving financial education assistance.

programs for the homeless. (See the Toolkit for a current list of VA programs.) Find partners to assist veterans who are struggling with financial issues.

- Find an organization or qualified volunteers to offer free income-tax-preparation assistance, financial literacy education, and information on asset building, which can go a long way toward help warriors gain and maintain self-sufficiency.

• Meaningful Employment

Providing employment coordination services will deliver a critical service that can empower warriors through a journey of self-sufficiency that creates economic well-being. Stable employment contributes to the financial security of warriors and their households. It enables them to meet their basic needs and focus on reintegration issues that may come up in the transition from military to civilian life or while dealing with physical and/or psychological wounds.

The following are the primary organizational expectations necessary to provide employment support to veterans seeking meaningful employment:

- Identify and develop partnerships with organizations that add value to each part of the employment spectrum, from résumé building to interview coaching, job fairs, networking events, affinity groups, diversity and inclusion, purposeful careers, and opportunities to give back to the community in which warriors live and work.

- Connect warriors seeking meaningful employment to available community employment resources.

- Connect warriors seeking meaningful employment to their state's VA office to apply for apprentice and on-the-job training programs.

- Assist warriors in applying for programs such as vocational rehabilitation and employment services.

- Address underemployment, vocational and trade needs, entrepreneurship, and other employment-related issues.

- Educate employers and businesses on the value of hiring a warrior.

Unemployment is a challenge facing many of our nation's citizens, but warriors comprise a uniquely valuable human resource talent pool entering America's labor force. Their training, education, skills, characteristics, and experiences are regularly unmatched. Yet, they are disproportionately unemployed when weighed against comparably qualified civilians. If appropriately assimilated into America's industries, warriors can help businesses attain higher financial goals, advance innovation, and grow into new markets, making our communities and nation stronger. The goal here is to shrink the gap that has formed between civilian workforces and transitioning warriors. When working with employers, instead of asking, "Will you hire veterans?" ask "Do you know the veterans who are working in your company?"

To meet your organization's employment objectives, you should consider applying the following strategies:

- Develop partnerships and collaborations with other organizations that encompass a wide range of topics, including the following:
  – Résumé preparation and translation of military skills
  – Vocational counseling and skills assessment
  – Education and advocacy
  – Mock interview workshops
  – Employment skills (networking skills, job search skills, job fairs skills, job readiness skills)
  – Financial or in-kind assistance for interview/work attire

These services will improve warriors' chances of becoming employed and successfully reintegrating into the communities to which they return home at the end of their military service.

- Develop partnerships with the employment services, staffing agencies, and companies within a community. You can begin by engaging organizations such as the following:
  – State department of labor
  – State employment security commission
  – Small business bureaus/alliances
  – Local work-study programs
  – Vocational rehabilitation
  – State department of social services

– Employment-focused nonprofits

– Top employers in the community

You want to ensure that these service agencies are aware of veteran challenges and are currently addressing the needs of this demographic.

The following are ways to facilitate this learning:

- Organize a job fair and invite local businesses, nonprofits, veterans services offices, and other service providers. In addition to being an excellent way to conduct outreach efforts, these events will also help your community raise awareness of the invaluable services offered by these organizations.

- Conduct local focus groups with employers, warriors, and community providers. You are sure to learn something that will help you improve your efforts to raise awareness with employers and provide employment coordination services to warriors and their family members.

• Education and Training

Education and training services provided to warriors will not only help you achieve your primary objective for education but will also indirectly assist you with the reduction of homelessness and unemployment among veterans, as well as reducing mental health needs. Education will change lives in innumerable ways, and in the current economic culture, it is a reliable predictor of a person's future employment, salary, and standard of living.

For veterans and their eligible family members, the post-9/11 GI Bill provides full tuition and fees for in-state public university students or gives a stipend based on the national maximum per academic year for out-of-state students or those enrolled in private schools. The post-9/11 GI Bill covers vocational, undergraduate, and graduate education as well as on-the-job training, licensing, flight training, and correspondence training. It includes funding for books, fees, and housing. (For more information, visit www.benefits.va.gov/gibill/.)

Despite this incredible benefit, challenges other than financial ones leave many post-9/11 veterans and their family members struggling with higher education. They are usually older; they may work, have dependents, struggle with invisible wounds, or feel it nearly impossible to navigate the bureaucracy of applying for and obtaining higher education. Communities owe it to veterans and their family members to assist them in eliminating these barriers.

The following are the basic organizational expectations necessary to support veterans seeking education and training:

- Partner with institutions of higher learning that want to change their culture on campus to be more accommodating, inviting, and empowering for veterans.
- Connect warriors with education needs to existing community educational resources.
- Work with local schools to conduct research on behalf of veterans' causes.
- Work with schools to engage with veterans utilizing vocational rehabilitation and post-9/11 GI Bill benefits.
- Work with education partners to ensure their staff is more culturally competent. Educate them about the value warrior students bring to the university and the unique challenges they face.
- Establish relationships with warrior students at colleges and technical schools, including frequent visits and physical availability on campus.

Through experience, America's Warrior Partnership has found that a successful strategy for improved outcomes in education and training is to assist local colleges and universities in becoming more warrior-friendly.

Creating a warrior-friendly educational institution is accomplished by

- collaborating with the schools to coordinate information about warriors seeking education and warriors already enrolled who need additional support; and
- supporting warriors as they navigate the education hurdles identified in your Community Assessment, which America's Warrior Partnership performs during your organization's development phase.

Whether your organization provides support for veterans in school via a hot desk at the local school or university or the educational institution has dedicated veteran advocates, it is essential to support and encourage veterans toward their ultimate education goal: not just enrolling but graduating.

TIPS
- ✪ If the school does not have a veterans' representative, advocate for and assist colleges and universities in the development of a veteran services department or veterans' representative who mentors warriors applying to or attending school.
- ✪ If the institution is unable to provide a veterans' representative, consider starting a support group for warrior students to attend on a weekly or biweekly basis, where they can get together and discuss common challenges and strategies to overcome them. This support group provides warriors with needed information and the opportunity to help others by sharing their success stories and tips. Support groups can also serve as an outreach tool and help eliminate the isolation that often accompanies the transition from military to civilian culture.

• Access to Earned Benefits

Accessing benefits empowers warriors to become financially secure and can put them on a path to economic well-being. By ensuring warriors can take full advantage of all government-provided benefits available to them, you help them secure a key component in their transition to life after military service. Because of the number of different organizations that provide benefits to individuals, depending on the warrior's situation, it can be confusing to figure out what the eligibility requirements are, how to apply, what types of documentation are needed when applying, and many other issues that arise when looking at benefit programs.

Whether you have an accredited benefits counselor on your staff or you partner with local government agencies or any other certified VSO, you will be working to support warriors as they access their earned benefits.

One of the issues with having so many benefits available is that it is difficult to track them and select which ones are appropriate for the situation. This is where a benefits counselor can help.

A successful benefits service counselor will assist warriors with the following:

- Determining eligibility and assisting with applications for federal or state benefits (federal disability compensation, pensions, education benefits, food stamps, and insurance)
- Enrolling warriors in the VA health-care system
- Making referrals to agencies that provide veteran-targeted programs (e.g., employment, homeownership, property tax exemption, motor vehicle registration)
- Providing legal guidance for appeals and disputes

NOTE: Warriors can receive free guidance from benefits counselors/ VSOs, but be aware that this is not the same as legal representation. Benefits counselors/VSOs cannot represent warriors in court; therefore, developing and maintaining a relationship with a local legal representative who has experience with veteran issues will enhance benefits counseling services. (See the Toolkit for information about a national pro bono legal service provider.)

To support warriors seeking access to earned benefits, your organization should consider applying the following strategies:

- Develop partnerships and collaborations with other organizations that provide benefits counseling, such as local veteran services agencies or any other certified VSO.
- Connect warriors with benefits needs to available community resources.
- Provide education to your organization's case coordinators so that they can work knowledgeably with individual warriors when providing information, counseling, assistance, and advocacy regarding their benefits, entitlements, and legal rights.
- Identify organizations that can assist with discharge upgrades or legal power of attorney (POA).

Some warriors may need additional legal support outside of discharge upgrades. The following are some strategies and tips to assist warriors who are seeking legal support services:

- Connect warriors with necessary and available legal assistance.
- Work with the local criminal justice system to educate personnel on issues specific to warriors.
- Identify and work with local veteran treatment court programs. Advocate for one in your area if needed. (The Toolkit contains information about developing a local veteran treatment court.)

TIPS ✪ Many communities have pro bono lawyers and law offices that would like to work with warriors on criminal, domestic, or civil disputes.
✪ Seek out community lawyers who have experience with upgrade and disability cases.
✪ Reach out to elected officials for assistance in finding legal and benefits support.
✪ See the Toolkit for a listing of national veteran legal service programs.

• Health

America's Warrior Partnership's goal is to maximize the level of health and wellness of warriors and their family members to increase their overall sense of well-being. The pursuit of health, personal growth, and improved quality of life relies on living a balanced life. To achieve balance, one needs to care for the mind, body, and spirit. If

any of these three areas are consistently lacking or forgotten about, the optimal level of health cannot be achieved.

Health care is a critical part of the holistic service model. It is an area where your organization will need to rely heavily on government, local VSOs, and local health-care support organizations to ensure that warriors and their family members have access to optimal health care. Your organization will be involved in connecting warriors to local VSOs that can assist them in registering with the VA or another health-care provider and additionally help them navigate insurance or insurance networks.

To support veterans, their families, and caregivers with physical, mental, and behavioral health, your organization should consider the following strategies:

 • Develop a relationship with your local VA and/or veterans center. It is vital that advocates know how to connect veterans to the wide variety of programs and services these organizations offer.

- Identify and connect with programs that positively and efficiently address posttraumatic stress, traumatic brain injury, major depression, moral injury or psychological trauma, posttraumatic growth, and sleep deprivation.

- Connect with organizations that have relationships with local veterans centers, VA medical centers, and counseling services. Work to improve accessibility, enrollment, and effectiveness in care.

EXAMPLES | – Finding a resource that assists the warrior with transportation for medical appointments.
– Finding a resource to assist with the pursuit of home remodeling made necessary by accessibility issues or finding organizations that will help pay for the remodeling.
– Assisting warriors to navigate available services, including obtaining and attending appointments and involving family members or caretakers as needed.

• Recreation:

Health is a dynamic process that it is always changing. As lifestyles and age change, so do levels of health. Those who participate in regular physical activity do so partly to improve the current and future level of their health but also to strive toward an optimal state of well-being. As lifestyles improve, health also improves, and less disease and sickness are experienced.

As a holistic case coordinator, your organization has a responsibility to guide and motivate warriors and their family members to improve their level of health and wellness.

Your organization can support warriors in maintaining optimal physical health by following these strategies:

 • Work with community partners to develop programs that give warriors an outlet to engage with their peers and to improve their health and well-being.

- Identify and connect warriors, their family members, and caregivers to recreational opportunities or social/physical health groups in the community. (See the Toolkit for a list of veteran recreational programs.)

- Advocate on behalf of warriors, their family members, and caregivers for free or reduced rates for participation in recreational, social, and physical activities.

- Create a community calendar of activities and opportunities and keep it up to date so that it becomes a useful tool for veterans and families.

- Advocate for warrior involvement in available nonclinical community physical wellness resources.

• Strong Family/Friend Relationships

As the saying goes, "No man is an island." It is essential for all people to surround themselves with family and friends for support and comfort in times of both joy and distress. Having supportive relationships is a strong protective factor against mental illnesses and helps to increase mental well-being.[5] In the veteran sphere, there is a growing body of evidence that effective family and couples' programs for returning veterans, especially veterans with posttraumatic stress disorder (PTSD), are an essential part of wellness and veteran support services.[6]

---

[5] C. A. Latkin and A. R. Knowlton, "Social Network Assessments and Interventions for Health Behavior Change: A Critical Review," *Behavioral Medicine* 41, no. 3 (2015): 90–97.

[6] L. W. Davis, R. Paul, D. Tarr, A. C. Eicher, J. Allinger, and H. Knock, "Operation Restoration: Couples Reunification Retreats for Veterans of Operations Enduring and Iraqi Freedom," *Journal of Psychosocial Nursing and Mental Health Services* 50 (2012): 20–29, http://dx.doi.org/10.3928/02793695- 20121003-02.

Your organization can support warriors, their families, and caregivers in building strong family and friend relationships by following these strategies:

- Partner with organizations that combat isolation, provide child care, offer marital counseling, provide outings with peer support, and provide consistent ways to engage and interact with one another in healthy ways.
- Connect warriors seeking family support with available community family support resources.
- Advocate for warrior involvement in existing nonclinical community peer support groups.

• Spirituality

In Dr. Steven Southwick's book *Resilience: The Science of Mastering Life's Greatest Challenges*, he describes how people overcome trauma, including war-induced trauma, through spirituality. He writes about spiritual people who find ways to "meet the challenge and continue with purposeful lives . . . they bounce back and carry on."[7] Spiritual well-being is deeply connected to emotional well-being and thus is integral to a veteran's quality of life.

Spirituality is a broad concept. It typically includes a connection to something bigger than oneself and a quest for a sense of purpose and meaning. People may seek spirituality support in places ranging from religious organizations to meditation groups or through mindfulness activities. Opportunities to explore spirituality are as varied as the nature of spirituality itself.

Your organization can support warriors seeking spirituality activities by enacting the following strategies:

- Partner with local churches and places of worship, and also partner with organizations that seek to address existential needs.
- Connect warriors seeking spiritual engagement with available community resources and opportunities.

---

[7] Steven M. Southwick and Dennis S. Charney, *Resilience: The Science of Mastering Life's Greatest Challenges* (New York: Cambridge University Press, 2018).

- Find opportunities for veterans to participate in meaningful activities to facilitate a sense purpose, a feeling of belonging, and a renewed identity.
- Advocate for warrior involvement in accessible nonclinical community spiritual wellness resources.

Serve Veterans through Partner Collaboration

Effective Community Integration programs coordinate leadership and recognize the strength in collaboration. Successful Community Integration programs have the following characteristics:

- Act as a clearinghouse to coordinate services and provide partner accountability.
- Act transparently in practices, partnerships, outreach, and financing.
- Avoid fragmentation by serving as the quarterback or convener while others specialize in services and provide those services well. Specializations in specific projects include adaptive housing and equipment, care packages for the homeless, child care, job mentoring, marital counseling, transportation services, legal assistance, and financial literacy, among others.
- Coordinate these partnerships into an organized and collaborative community prepared to meet warriors' needs. Allow veterans service organizations, local businesses, local policymakers, and community members to collectively surround warriors with these resources by expanding the reach and scope of programs and services.

Collaborate with other Organizations

Collaboration is a best practice for any organization that is the leader for warrior care in its community. Through collaboration, you build strong community partner relationships at both a direct-service level and a management level. You build bridges that ensure your organization is involved in identifying, addressing, and solving community concerns.

The following are recommended practices when seeking to collaborate with other community organizations:

- Focus on consumer services, not what each partner organization will get out of it. Your best reward for collaboration is giving the best possible help to the warriors in your community.

- Establish a specific point person or point of contact for consumer services at each partner agency, and encourage staff from each agency to build a strong working relationship.

- Establish a "hot desk," a physical space at partner locations in the community where you can meet with warriors and be available for outreach or for partner staff to communicate and collaborate.

- Take the lead in initiating referrals for partner services; however, take the time to build a good working relationship before you send large volumes of referrals to a partner.

- Establish open and honest communication between organizations at the management level.

- Offer value to your partners through the process of referring customers. Sending and receiving qualified referrals helps improve metrics for both organizations. Giving good service to the referrals you receive shows respect to your referring partner. Offering referrals to your partners shows you trust them to do good work.

- Offer your organization's help and resources to other groups in your community when they ask for help, when you are part of a group addressing a challenge, or when you have extra resources (staff time, expertise, donated items, etc.) that you can share.

- Continually update your Community Profile Map using publicly accessible data to assess your community and understand its gaps and barriers. Use this data to help drive your outreach and engagement with veterans and community organizations. By updating this map frequently, it becomes a dynamic resource for any staff and volunteers who work directly with your community's veterans, providing them with current information about local service providers.

TIP America's Warrior Partnership has developed a community connector program, called the Network, that connects community organizations to national service partners; educates communities and partners about solving problems beyond the community's means through close communication; advocates for the veteran and the community through case coordination; provides data analytics on gaps, trends, issues, social predictors, and indicators; and collaborates broadly with national partners and community organizations.

A hallmark of America's Warrior Partnership's model is the belief that resources already exist in every community to serve warriors. Your organization must use already-available resources whenever possible. If you ignore existing services and insist on reinventing the wheel or duplicating programs, you will do the following:

✳ Waste time, energy, money, and human capital

✳ Show a lack of trust and faith in other service organizations

✳ Insult other organizations by taking away their opportunity to succeed in their service area

✳ Appear arrogant and unwilling to work with others

✳ Appear unconnected to and ignorant about what is going on in your community

✳ Turn off funders and supporters who recognize the benefits of collaboration and cooperation

✳ Run the risk of missing the chance to provide the best possible services for the warriors in your community

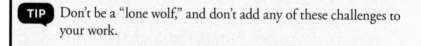

TIP Don't be a "lone wolf," and don't add any of these challenges to your work.

LEADING THE COMMUNITY

As the lead agency for warrior case coordination within your community, not only should your agency act as the go-to agency on warrior issues and care, but also your agency should be the nexus of the warrior-centric network that you will be building through Community Integration.

How Does Our Organization Become the Lead Organization for Warrior Issues?

Step 1: Study the Community Analysis completed by America's Warrior Partnership. It is a good idea to go into the initial community meeting armed with relevant information about the strengths and weaknesses of your community. A savvy leader always knows the correct answer before he or she poses the question.

Step 2: Conduct a Community Roundtable
As you begin a Community Integration initiative, it is helpful to conduct a roundtable-style meeting at which you gather many service providers together to identify the current services available, what each service does, and what resources are missing in the community. The Community Profile Map completed by America's Warrior Partnership is an excellent resource for invitees.

TIPS ✪ Offering a free lunch as part of the meeting is a good way to entice many people to attend.
✪ Work with your America's Warrior Partnership support staff; they can help with tips and advice on how to make your roundtable go smoothly.

Step 3: Begin Warrior Outreach and Advocacy
After these initial roundtables, you will likely want to focus on your outreach and advocacy efforts with warriors for a short period to establish your credibility as a leader in the community.

Step 4: Convene Groups to Address Community Needs or Challenges
When you have a track record of accomplishments as a service provider and a community partner, you will be able to use your position as the community's warrior services leader to convene groups to address community needs or challenges.

Partner Accountability

Build relationships with community organizations genuinely vested in warriors' success, whether they are affinity groups of corporations, employers, education institutions, VA or military installation points of contact, and so forth, and hold them accountable. Maintain a role in the execution of promised services, from referral to task completion. Connect with both the organization providing the service and the warrior to determine the efficacy of assistance.[8]

What makes a worthy partner?
- A defined mission and allegiance to that mission
- Financially responsible and sustainable for the long haul
- Trusted by warriors
- Respected in the community
- Transparent in all aspects of operations
- Has a system for measuring impact

Community Partners

Building relationships with community partners and leveraging their resources as part of a holistic plan to serve veterans and their families is a critical component of the Community Integration model. The following paragraphs list potential community partners and essential activities associated with quality service delivery. Consider using this list as a guide to assist you in identifying exceptional community partners.

---

[8] P. Carter and K. Kidder, "A Continuum of Collaboration," last modified April 2017, https://www.cnas.org/publications/reports/a-continuum-of-collaboration.

Housing partners link veterans and their family members to emergency shelter, transitional housing, supportive housing, and independent housing options to establish housing stability.

In addition to having the partner accountability qualities listed previously, a quality housing partner should do the following:
- Understand what services and grants are provided by your local VA office, including the HUD-VASH program, and stay up to date on eligibility requirements.
- Expand awareness of homelessness and housing issues in the community.
- Perform warrior screening for housing needs and review applicants for suitability and eligibility for specific programs.
- Participate as an active member of the continuum of care.

Employment partners provide supportive services to increase the ability of veterans and their family members to obtain and maintain meaningful employment so that they can achieve economic well-being and self-sufficiency.

In addition to having the accountability qualities of a worthy partner, a quality employment partner should do the following:
- Conduct assessments, review documentation, and provide situational vocational evaluations that identify the strengths and needs of warriors relating to employment.
- Assist individual warriors in the job-search process and provide the required support, including completion/review of applications, networking with prospective employers, mock interviews, and guidance with any preemployment paperwork or online application processes.
- Provide information and assistance with résumés.
- Provide positive reinforcement for desired behavior and promote social integration, worker socialization, proper communication skills, and positive work attitudes.
- Conduct employment workshops.
- Engage and participate in job fairs.
- Maintain a job database and provide appropriate job leads to warriors.

Education partners serve as a nexus of higher learning institutions comprising local universities, community colleges, and technical institutes.

In addition to having the accountability qualities of a worthy partner, a quality education partner should have the following:

- A veteran services department or veterans' representative who mentors warriors applying to or attending school

  This mentor should do the following:
  - Provide warriors with accurate and up-to-date information on the different categories of educational benefits for which they may apply.
  - Assist warriors in navigating the submission process for the VA GI Bill educational certificate of eligibility (COE), or help with VA work-study programs or referrals to vocational rehabilitation for educational assistance.
  - Provide guidance on selecting a program of study based on a warrior's qualifications, needs, and desires.
  - Develop and maintain an extensive educational plan for each warrior student.
  - Identify and follow all warrior students to ensure they are maximizing their educational benefits and will complete their education program.
  - Keep warriors informed of changes in educational benefits and policies.

Benefits partners offer veterans benefits assistance and counseling. Health-care systems serving warriors can be disjointed, as well as time-consuming and exasperating to navigate. Research has shown that personalized assistance is beneficial in ensuring enrollment in or receipt of benefits.

In addition to having the accountability qualities of a worthy partner, a quality benefits partner should do the following:

- Assist warriors in navigating through the submission process for their benefits claims, ensuring that comprehensive claims are submitted.

- Follow up after benefit-claim submission for status updates from warriors.
- Assist warriors in applying for appeals and changes in discharge status.
- Coordinate with VSOs and VA administrators to ensure warriors are receiving accurate information related to benefits eligibility and applications.
- Maintain continuing education relevant to current information regarding warrior entitlement benefits.
- Provide warriors with accurate and up-to-date information on specific benefits and entitlements (e.g., service-connected disability, non-service-connected disability, and Social Security).

Health-care partners may be health-care providers, counselors, or mental health clinicians. They are the resident experts to help warriors navigate and access appropriate health-care resources. Please be sure that only properly trained and certified individuals provide professional or clinical mental health services. Noncertified individuals may only provide outreach, advocacy, navigation, encouragement, and general support for warriors who are seeking professional assistance.

In addition to having the accountability qualities of a worthy partner, a quality health-care partner should do the following:

- Network with community members, VA offices, veterans centers, and other mental health programs to ensure community-wide marketing of these programs.
- Assist warriors to navigate available services, including obtaining and attending appointments and involving family members or caretakers as needed.
- Assist warriors with connecting to mental health providers for services when needed.

Financial services partners are the resident experts to help warriors navigate and access financial education assistance resources, which is essential when providing holistic support.

In addition to having the accountability qualities of a worthy partner, a quality financial services partner should do the following:

- Network with community members, consumer credit assistance programs, homeownership programs, and other financial education programs to ensure the programs are marketed to warriors community-wide.
- Facilitate financial literacy workshops.

Legal services partners are the resident experts to help warriors navigate and access legal assistance resources.

In addition to having the accountability qualities of a worthy partner, a quality legal services partner should do the following:

- Network with community members and state and local legal aid programs.
- Assist warriors to navigate the legal system and available services.

Spirituality/recreational partners assist warriors by addressing the existential, communal, and physical activity needs of warriors. They provide veterans with opportunities to participate in meaningful activities, facilitating a sense of purpose, a feeling of belonging, and a renewed identity, and provide an outlet to engage with their peers and improve their health and well-being.

In addition to having the accountability qualities of a worthy partner, a quality spiritual/recreational partner should do the following:

- Conduct outreach to warriors seeking spiritual and recreational activities.
- Network with community members and recreational and spiritual programs to ensure the programs are marketed to warriors community-wide.

Several national organizations provide peer mentoring to warriors in specific locations or via phone or online connections. (See the Toolkit for a list of peer mentor organizations.)

Manage Your Resources on a Local Level

Nationally, it has been argued that the "sea of goodwill" comprises anywhere between forty and forty-five thousand nonprofit organizations devoted to veteran causes in this country. What our efforts and supporting studies have shown is that veterans do better when the community has a collective model in place.[9] Nonprofits can adapt to the changing needs of the community faster than government agencies. You should work to complement and augment the government's programs and services. When identifying key partners locally, regionally, and nationally, we have learned it is critical to know your backyard. Many times, national umbrella organizations have chapters and affiliates across the country. Understand the national organizations' accountability structure. We cannot stress enough the importance of exhausting accessible resources locally before you reach for national aid and assistance. Communities need to be vested in warriors' best interests.

The following are strategies to encourage successful collaborative services:

- Move away from separate data-management systems if possible. Use a common information technology platform like WarriorServe® to track warriors' progress and placement in the community and to communicate with fellow agencies.

- Attend/host conferences and events that expand your knowledge base and keep your work current and relevant to warriors' wants and needs. Stay within your nonprofit's charter to prevent mission creep.

- Never develop programming in a vacuum. Go directly to the source (i.e., the constituency you serve) to see if your vision is in line with their vision.

- Remain versatile and cooperative. Recognize that warrior goals or community goals may change over time according to community needs.

---

[9]Office of the Chairman of the Joint Chiefs of Staff, Office of Reintegration, "After the Sea of Goodwill: A Collective Approach to Veteran Reintegration," last modified October 2014, http://www.jcs.mil/Portals/36/Documents/CORe/After_the_Sea_of_Goodwill.pdf.

CHAPTER HIGHLIGHTS

 Outreach is an action that can only be achieved by going out into the community.

 To connect with veterans, you must find them through outreach, get to know them by completing an intake assessment, and create a holistic plan to support them in goal achievement.

 To become the lead veteran organization in your community, you must engage in proactive community outreach.

 All warriors' needs can be reached by collaborating with existing resource providers and working in concert with the community to fill gaps in services.

 Building trusted relationships with warriors is vital for a successful Community Integration program. Trust is built one step at a time and sustained through regular communications and being true to your word.

CHAPTER 4:
SETTING UP YOUR TEAM

What's in this chapter?

✓ Details about specific roles and tasks in your organization that are essential for the implementation of Community Integration

✓ Specific information regarding volunteers

✓ Models of effective organizational structures for start-up, young, and mature organizations following the Community Integration model

"The secret to success is good leadership, and good leadership is all about making the lives of your team members or workers better."

~ Tony Dungy,
retired NFL Coach

Team Overview

When designing your organizational structure, it is essential to understand your community. You should:

✓ Learn and understand the culture of your community.

✓ Know who are the key leaders/players and organizations/providers in the community.

✓ Strive to not duplicate quality services already existing in your community. No single organization can be a subject-matter expert in all services and needs.

Once you have familiarized yourself with the landscape of your community (your Community Profile Map is a good starting point for this process), you can begin to identify gaps in services so that you can leverage existing resources and determine how to address any deficiencies.

Keep in mind that your organization's role within your community is to connect, educate, advocate and collaborate!

ORGANIZATIONAL STRUCTURE

A fundamental concept to remember as you plan your organizational chart for warrior services is that your most important responsibility is proactive outreach. Be sure to also focus your staffing power on engagement and case coordination with warriors. Rely on other community partners to provide direct services in their areas of expertise.

Some communities will find it better to offer all services based under a single roof by way of inviting collaborating agencies to share space with them, whereas others will seek to place team members in other agencies' offices.

• Whenever possible, keep overhead down by using spaces provided at little or no cost by partner agencies or supporters. Often, schools, hospitals, other nonprofits, and military facilities will provide space if you serve their clients.

- No matter how well placed your offices are, outreach occurs in the community, not behind a desk.

In the Beginning

You only need two people to start Community Integration: the executive director and another staff member. Personalities and abilities will determine the roles and responsibilities.

EXAMPLE

One person will need to focus on case coordination.

- Their first task is to build partnerships with existing resources in the community.
- This person will work to identify viable services that meet the needs of veterans and their families/caregivers in the eight areas of holistic support described in chapter 3.
- It is this person's responsibility to provide case coordination between partner services for veterans as they identify their needs. Responsibilities include the following:
- Referring warriors to partners for assistance
- Following up with partners to ensure that warriors are receiving appropriate services
- Following up with warriors to see if their needs were met or if they have additional needs

 TIP If your organization is following America's Warriors Partnership's Community Integration model, see your Community Profile Map for help with this task.

The second person will focus on proactive outreach.

- Their first task is to build social media presence and start engaging with the community.
- Next, this person will conduct outreach to warriors by creating opportunities for them to connect with your organization and with other warriors in the community.
- This person should use the direct method of outreach by attending

events or visiting locations frequented by veterans.

- This person should also use the indirect method by building relationships with other organizations, other than direct-service providers, that will speak out about your organization and will refer veterans to you.

Outreach is not an easy task. You must be out and about in the community as much as possible to meet your outreach goals. To avoid stepping on each other's toes, establish which organizations the "case coordination" person will build a relationship with and which organizations the "outreach" person will build a relationship with. Proper communication internally will mitigate the risk of overlapping efforts.

Additionally, the two roles may need to take on additional responsibilities, described later in the section "Team Roles and Tasks," depending on the size of your organization.

It is vital to ensure you are staying focused on the Community Integration model while increasing your team by doing the following:

- Focus your energy on case coordination and outreach.

- Find partnering agencies that can provide direct services. Use your employees for case coordination and outreach instead.

Emerging Community Integration Organization

As your organization matures, you will likely need to expand your staff.

- To increase your case-coordination and outreach efforts, you may need to hire a lead in these two areas. You may also discover you need to add specific team members to meet the roles and tasks described in the next section.

- In terms of veteran needs, 80 percent of the veteran population has few needs, whereas 20 percent of the population has multiple or complex needs. Therefore, it is the outreach team's responsibility to find all veterans and regularly engage with the 80 percent of the veterans who have few needs. Although the case coordinators may work with most veterans, they will spend most of their time with the 20 percent of warriors who have multiple or complex needs. As a result, your outreach team will be larger than your case-coordination team.

SETTING UP YOUR TEAM—TEAM ROLES AND TASKS

The following are examples of duties and responsibilities for service team members in administering the Community Integration model approach to helping warriors. You may find that a specific position is not necessary in your organization because other staff members or community organizations can handle the task.

Although each Community Integration organization will have different strengths and places where help is needed, all eight areas must be addressed for holistic service provision to occur.

To be effective and achieve your organization's Community Integration goals, you will want to ensure that your organization has the following:

- A robust outreach program
- A comprehensive assessment plan for all warriors
- A strategy for the coordination of services with follow-up

The goal is to provide a well-rounded approach to warriors' support so that they receive individualized service coordination and care. This holistic approach will ensure they can set and attain goals that improve their well-being.

In addition to using existing community resources as much as possible, you may find that leveraging other assets in lieu of full-time employees may be the best fit to address specific areas within your organization or community.

Probable people assets are as follows:
- Volunteers
- Interns
- National volunteer organizations (See the Toolkit for specific information.)

The Face of the Program

Typically, the face of the program is the executive director, program director/lead, or another staff member, depending on program maturity. This individual is the head administrative officer of your warrior service program and is accountable for achieving the program's mission and financial objectives. Responsibilities include but are not limited to the following:

- Ensuring that the organization has a long-range strategy to accomplish its mission and incremental steps planned to ensure consistent and timely progress

- Providing leadership in development and implementation of the program's organizational and financial plans with the board of directors and staff

- Promoting active and broad participation by volunteers in all areas of the organization's work

- Maintaining official records and documents; ensuring compliance with federal, state, and local regulations; and maintaining a working knowledge of significant developments and trends in the field

- Establishing sound working relationships and cooperative arrangements with community groups and organizations

- Representing the program and point of view of the organization to agencies, organizations, and the general public

- Possessing comprehensive knowledge of military service and the US Department of Veterans Affairs (VA) system

Boots on the Ground—Case Coordination

The case coordinator serves as the primary point of implementation for the program services received by warriors and their family members. This person works directly with warriors and their family members in achieving their goals. Duties include but are not limited to the following:

- Conducting intake and assessments with individuals to discover needs and developing a holistic warrior care plan that will guide the delivery of services and resources

- Advocating for warriors by assisting in the expansion of community resources and maintaining cooperative relationships with community groups, partners, and resource agencies
- Developing and maintaining a system of referrals across a broad spectrum of agencies, including medical, nonprofit, and government agencies
- Ensuring that direct-service partners are providing comprehensive warrior care to veterans receiving assistance according to their holistic warrior care plans
- Updating warrior records to include eligibility documents, assessment forms, information and referral logs, case notes, volunteer and donation logs, surveys, and other records as assigned
- Conducting meetings with warriors, retirees, and family members throughout the community to discuss VA benefits and programs

Boots on the Ground—Outreach

 The outreach specialist is responsible for building and maintaining relationships with warriors and their family members. They oversee outreach opportunities within the community.

Duties include the following:

- Coordinating, developing, implementing, and maintaining a wide range of community outreach events and programs for warriors
- Establishing and maintaining contact with local colleges' staff and faculty, military and VA hospitals' staff, directors of military retirement/transition services, local department of labor offices, local public libraries, community-based organizations, and warriors
- Assisting in the development of community events designed to educate warriors about opportunities in their community and educate the community about the value of warriors
- Developing and maintaining cooperative relationships with community groups, partners, and resource agencies
- Ensuring accurate initial intake information is gathered so that the case coordinators can follow up

- Engaging in community outreach efforts to recruit volunteers and college outreach efforts to recruit interns
- Creating volunteer opportunities and managing volunteers in the field

> **TIP** We have found that veterans make awesome "boots on the ground" as case coordinators or outreach specialists. Those who have served military veterans and their families over the years will claim this role becomes the greatest honor of their lives. Many of those who have served in the military (veterans or family members) choose to continue to give back to their fellow brothers and sisters in arms in their community. Keeping warriors the focal point of your everyday work is essential. In order to best serve veterans, community organizations must build partnerships that embody service and accountability to veterans. We believe all veterans should be known; that each veteran should be served, both individually and holistically; and that all veterans should have an elevated hope and purpose. Becoming a case coordinator in a veteran-serving organization can provide the veteran an opportunity to continue their service.

The Messenger

The messenger is responsible for creating and delivering marketing programs, activities, and materials. The messenger manages projects and ensures your organization's message is consistent and aligned with the branding requirements of your organization and your partners.

Duties include the following:
- Creating, delivering, and optimizing marketing materials that are supportive of and consistent with the organization's marketing strategies
- Leading social media outreach efforts and delivering content via appropriate platforms (e.g., Facebook, Twitter, LinkedIn, email, direct mail)

- Creating and delivering press releases, media relations content, newsletter/annual report content, social media content, digital media content, and speaking proposals according to approved plan/strategy
- Identifying, developing, and executing communications strategy for key media contacts and warrior references
- Researching media coverage and industry trends
- Managing and curating video content and other digital media content
- Regularly updating content on the organization's website and social media presence

Development

 The development specialist is responsible for assisting the executive director or program director in obtaining financial support for program operations. He or she participates in fundraising, grant writing, and corporate sponsorship development.

Duties include the following:

- Adhering to approved development and grant-writing calendars for timely execution of assigned development tasks
- Creating and delivering appropriate fundraising documents and grant proposals
- Researching prospective grantors and donors and retaining and sharing appropriate information about potential supporters with leadership staff and board members as needed
- Conducting approved fundraising campaigns seeking financial support from individuals and companies
- Collecting statistical information about outcomes, services, and program achievements and using the information to garner support for your organization
- Ensuring donors are thanked and recognized appropriately and in a timely fashion
- Keeping accurate and complete records of donations received and donor wishes for recognition

- Providing donation information as needed for annual reports and other required uses

The Steward—Bookkeeper

 The steward is responsible for assisting the executive director or program director in managing the finances and operations budget for the program. The steward participates in budgeting, financial management, human resources, and operations.

Duties include the following:

- Ensuring programs are meeting budget expectations and acting as a liaison between the accounting firm and the organization

- Managing human resources and day-to-day operations within the organization, including securing legal documentation necessary for staff, interns, and volunteers

- Identifying areas where volunteer work could extend the reach of your mission and implementing a screening process to ensure the matching of volunteers to appropriate opportunities

- Creating written job descriptions for staff and volunteer assignments

- Training and managing volunteers for the specific areas where they will help, which may include confidentiality training, peer mentor training, or other specific needs (Supervision of the intern will fall under the intern's academic specialty.)

- Keeping records of staff and volunteer time and tasks and using the tracked information to match grants and leverage other donations; can be done with software programs that allow staff and volunteers to track their hours and manage their availability

 TIP In the beginning, the development and steward positions could be 1099 independent contractors or pro bono volunteers.

Service Partners—Part of Your Team

Don't forget to recognize partners as a part of your team. Partners are responsible for delivering direct services to address warriors' needs, as described in chapter 3. Case coordinators should have a close working relationship with service providers to ensure warriors are receiving the services they need promptly. Partner duties are as follows:

- Assisting warriors with one or more of the following:
  - Finding permanent housing
  - Finding meaningful employment
  - Maintaining strong family and friend relationships
  - Obtaining education and training
  - Accessing earned benefits
  - Receiving physical, mental, and behavioral health care
  - Accessing recreational and spiritual opportunities
  - Building, reinforcing, and managing their finances
  - Conducting outreach to warriors and educating them about your organization's services

Board of Directors/Advisory Board—Part of Your Team

Your board of directors and/or advisory board is a valuable part of your organization's team. These boards can serve in a variety of roles to support your success. Board member and officer roles should have a job description that specifies the responsibilities and time commitment expected. Your organization bylaws should also provide requirements and specifics for the board member/director and board officer roles. Remember that the bylaws legally govern your organization and take precedence over other descriptions of board responsibilities.

The following are qualities or skills that board members should possess:

- They should have a diverse background and have familiarity with a variety of industries within your community.

- They have many community contacts and can assist with networking and creating connections for projects, plans, information, or collaboration.

- They are donors who provide financial support for your organization and invite others to give financial resources.

- They are volunteers in their board role but may also want to serve as hands-on volunteers working directly with warriors.

- They can educate their community contacts on warriors' needs and recruit volunteers or in-kind donations to meet known needs.

- They serve as another set of eyes and ears for your organization. They can help ensure documents or projects that will face the public are on point, understandable, and organized before being released. They also are likely to become aware of any concerns, confusion, or miscommunication about your organization in the community before your staff hears about it.

- Remember that your board members are volunteers and should be appreciated and recognized for sharing their time, talent, treasure, and influence with your organization.

Volunteers—Part of Your Team

Employees are a significant expense for nonprofits. Consider using volunteers for tasks that do not require paid employees.

Guidelines and considerations for volunteers include the following:

- Volunteers are typically unpaid, part-time workers who bring their time, talents, and often, their financial support to help achieve the organization's mission.

- Volunteers can do simple tasks such as answer phones or file paperwork. You may find some volunteers that have particular expertise and can work on an as-needed basis and assist with community outreach, as well as capacity building.

- Volunteers always require supervision and attention.

TIPS

✪ If the family member of an employee expresses a desire to volunteer, it is important to place the volunteer in a position where he or she does not work with and is not supervised by the family member.

✪ Take a cautious approach when considering current or former warrior clients as volunteers. Even though they may want to help other veterans by volunteering for the organization that helped them, if the veteran has a recent history of health or mental health struggles or homelessness, it might be best for him or her to have a period of recovery before working in highly stressful areas of the organization.

- Volunteers are an investment because they can make your organization better. Their expertise, understanding, skill, and contacts can enhance your overall effort.
- Volunteers help increase the likelihood that your efforts will be sustainable.

Interns—Part of Your Team

Internships are formal agreements with academic institutions that allow your organization to leverage intelligent undergraduate or graduate students.

- Many professions require an internship, a period of supervised training, as part of their curriculum.
- Internship opportunities can build capacity while simultaneously contributing to the growth, professional development, and education of your community by taking an active role in the training of future professionals.
- Many university social work programs have specific tracks for working within the area of the military, veterans, and their families that prepare students to do the following:
  - Assist service members, veterans, and their families with the stresses of military life and transition.
  - Help community-based agencies identify and serve military populations in their community.
- The number of hours per week and the length of time an intern is assigned to your organization may differ, depending on the professions involved, the student's degree program, and the student's year of study.
- Internships are typically unpaid positions.
- Having interns is a serious commitment of time and effort. You must provide a solid learning experience and follow all school guidelines for the internship.

> **TIP** Savvy use of interns can generate an exponential increase in your outreach and engagement efforts. Instead of sending one staff member with a Master of Social Work degree out to do five hours of outreach, consider having your staff member supervise two master's level interns with that time, each of whom is performing ten hours of outreach per week.

ORGANIZATIONAL CHARTS

The following are conceptual organizational charts for a small/start-up, maturing, and mature nonprofit organization following America's Warrior Partnership's Community Integration model.

The icons represent the recommended roles/task for each person

 Everyone on the team is responsible for outreach.

SMALL OR START-UP VETERAN-CENTRIC NONPROFIT WITH 2 STAFF MEMBERS

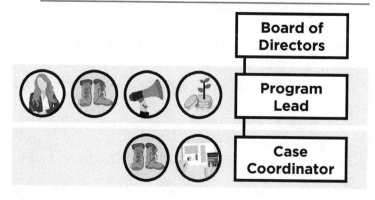

MATURING VETERAN-CENTRIC NONPROFIT

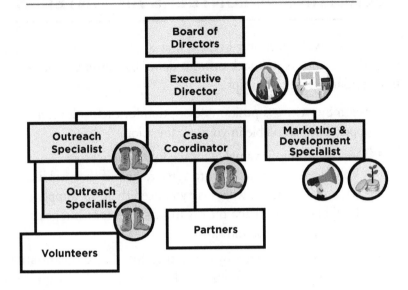

MATURE VETERAN-CENTRIC NONPROFIT

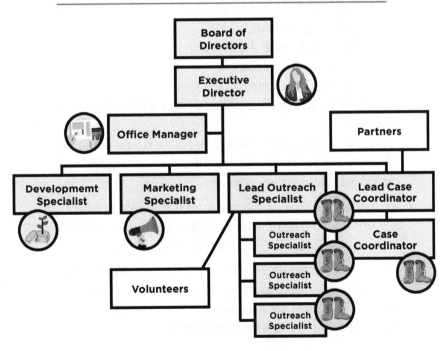

RECRUITING VOLUNTEERS AND INTERNS

Many people volunteer only because they are asked. Do not wait for potential volunteers to knock on your door. To recruit volunteers, you must initiate the relationships.

- Begin by writing a position description for each volunteer opportunity available in your organization.
- This description is valuable for the following reasons:
  - Volunteers are more likely to agree to help if they feel like they have a clear idea of what task you need them to complete.
  - It will help you match the organization's needs and goals with a volunteer's interest and skills.
- You can find volunteers by contacting faith-based organizations, other nonprofits, local groups such as Veterans of Foreign Wars (VFW), the American Legion, family readiness groups (FRGs), universities and colleges, and government agencies.
- Veterans and their family members often make amazing volunteers for the following reasons:
  - They have skill sets and characteristics that are highly desirable for employees and volunteers.
  - They are loyal, accountable, service oriented, and adaptable, and they understand the military culture from their firsthand experiences.
  - They are waiting to be asked and have a strong desire to serve.
  - Volunteering is an excellent way for them to acquire civilian experience for later employment.
- Stay connected to your volunteers even if you do not have opportunities in the near future. These volunteers may be necessary for future events or may become donors.
- Keep records of volunteer/intern times and tasks. Use this information to match grants and leverage other donations. Software programs are available that allow the volunteers to track their hours and manage their availability.

- Recognize volunteer efforts. Implement an annual appreciation event or recognition award so that volunteers know they are valued and understand the impact they bring to the organization and to the warriors they serve.

How Can My Organization Host an Intern?

1. First, engage the institution and department of learning that you wish to use (i.e., for a social work intern, contact the department of social work of the college or university).

2. Give the institution a profile of your organization, an outline of the learning opportunities to be provided (see the Toolkit for an example outline), and a résumé of the qualified personnel who will be the intern's direct supervisor.

3. If selected as a learning site, you will have an opportunity to interview interns to be sure you are getting a "good fit."

4. If you and the selected intern are in agreement and he or she will be assigned to your organization, you will be expected to sign a contract or memorandum of agreement (MOA).

5. Give interns real projects. They should not be used to do manual labor, run errands, or conduct administrative duties unrelated to their degree field.

TIP Read the MOA over carefully to ensure that the requirements of the educational institution and the learning objectives of the student are in accordance with the mission of your organization and that the responsibilities of the internship provide an opportunity for the student to meet his or her learning objectives. It is imperative that the community organization provides supervision and oversight, ensuring the student completes the learning objectives and goals.

CHAPTER HIGHLIGHTS

 Small nonprofit organizations, with only two staff members, are able to begin a Community Integration program.

 To be effective, you will want to ensure that your organization has the following:

* A robust outreach program
* A comprehensive assessment plan for all warriors
* A strategy for the coordination of services with follow-up

 The outreach team will find all veterans and regularly engage with the 80 percent of the veterans who have few needs. The case coordinators will spend most of their time with the 20 percent of warriors who have multiple or complex needs. As a result, your outreach team will be larger than your case-coordination team.

 In addition to using existing community resources as much as possible, you may find that leveraging other assets in lieu of full-time employees may be the best fit to address specific areas within your organization or community.

CHAPTER 5:
CRAFTING AND TRACKING OUTCOMES

What's in this chapter?

✓ Why metrics are vital to your nonprofit

✓ Why writing goals, objectives, and outcomes is necessary and how to do so

✓ Example goals and objectives based on the principles of Community Integration

✓ Best practices for tracking outcomes

"Life's most persistent and urgent question is, 'What are you doing for others?'"

~ Martin Luther King, Jr.

OUTCOME OVERVIEW

Every veteran service organization should be prepared to report on its successes using measurable outcomes.

Outcomes have the following characteristics:
- They are the evidence of a nonprofit organization's success.
- They are the expression of the motives that drive a nonprofit's mission.
- They provide an organization with proof of its value to existing funders, potential funders, and the broader community.
- They are important quantifiable performance measures. (This is especially vital in the increasingly competitive social service industry.)

The difference between goals, objectives, and outcomes is often perplexing. In fact, if you search, you will often see the terms used inconsistently. Betsy Baker offers an excellent explanation in her article "How to Write Goals, Objectives and Outcomes That Grant Funders Will Love!":

EXAMPLE | While a goal gives a general statement of your program's purpose, objectives are more concrete and specific in how the goal will be achieved. Your outcomes should reflect the expected results at the end of your proposal's project period.[10]

The following list notes the goal, objectives, and an outcome for a grant application written by a fictitious veteran-focused community service program, known as Warrior Community Solutions, that targets veterans who are seeking education and assists them with enrollment and support:

- Goal: Warrior Community Solutions will assist veterans seeking education to obtain their earned education benefits and provide the support and assistance they need to graduate.

---

[10]Betsy Baker, "How to Write Goals, Objectives and Outcomes That Grant Funders Will Love," Grant Professionals Association, last modified January 3, 2012, https://www.grantprofessionals.org/rc_files/27/How_to_Write_Goals_Objectives_and_Outcomes_-_Betsy_Baker.pdf.

- Objective 1: Warrior Community Solutions will assist fifty veterans each year in applying for their earned education benefits.
- Objective 2: Of the veterans enrolled in the college and in need of transportation to get back and forth to class, 100 percent will be provided taxi or gas vouchers.
- Outcome: Of all veterans participating in Warrior Community Solutions education program, 90 percent will obtain a degree.

WRITING GOALS, OBJECTIVES, AND OUTCOMES

Goal—A goal is a broad, overarching mission that you hope to accomplish. It is a statement about the impact your organization wishes to make.

Example Goal: Warrior Community Solutions will improve the lives of veterans by connecting them to the resources that they are seeking.

Objectives—Objectives are measurable, concrete, and specific steps in how the goal will be achieved. They are explicit targets that support your goal.

Example Objective 1: Warrior Community Solutions will establish relationships with one hundred veterans each month as measured by the data entered into WarriorServe®.

Example Objective 2: Within a year, 80 percent of all veterans seeking employment will be employed as measured by the data entered into WarriorServe®.

Outcomes—Outcomes provide the measurable intended results your organization will accomplish at the end of a given amount of time.

An outcome should have two parts:
1. A prediction of results
2. A measurement method to determine whether each outcome has been achieved

The Community Foundation of the Central Savannah River Area

offers a succinct explanation of outcomes on its website:

> Outcomes are the benefits and/or changes that occur in individuals or groups as a **result of their participation** in a program or activity. Outcomes can involve knowledge, skills, attitudes, behavior, performance, status or condition. **Do not confuse outcomes with broad or vague statements or with counting program activities.**[11]

Statements such as "Post-9/11 veterans will feel more empowered" are ambiguous and too broad to be acceptable outcomes. Likewise, just describing the amount of service delivered (e.g., the number of homeless veterans who have been housed) does not demonstrate what benefits the participants gained from the program.

> Example Outcome: As a result of improved engagement due to the creation of one hundred new outreach events and the support of other events via advertising, invitation, and attendance, 85 percent of known veterans within the organization's catchment area will report feeling a sense of well-being as measured by America's Warrior Partnership's annual survey.

Measurable outcomes will answer the following questions:
- The creation of what? (improved engagement due to the creation of one hundred outreach events and support of other events)
- To assist who and how many of whom? (all known veterans within the catchment area)
- To do what? (report a sense of well-being)
- By how much? (85 percent)
- Using what tool? (annual survey)
- When? (yearly)

Outcome measurement is an unbiased way to assess the extent to which your veteran program is successful.

The central questions answered by outcomes are as follows:
- What has changed in the lives of veterans, their family members, and caregivers because of your program?

---

[11]The Community Foundation, "Grant Seeker Guidelines," last modified 2018, http://www.cfcsra.org/GrantSeekerGuidelines.

- Has your program made a difference in the community?
- How are the lives of veterans, their family members, and caregivers better because of your program?

America's Warrior Partnership's Metrics

America's Warrior Partnership utilizes common metrics to measure the overall success of organizations following the Community Integration model. The metrics were selected to support a holistic model of warrior support and represent concepts that resonate with healthy communities at large. Due to the diversity of communities, it is important to use standardized metrics to ensure an unbiased measure of community health and to quantify the successful outcomes of warrior-centric organizations.

Community Integration's Goals, Objectives, and Intended Outcomes

America's Warrior Partnership helps each organization following the Community Integration model develop its own measurable objectives based on America's Warrior Partnership's goals, which are derived from the common metrics.

These objectives have the following characteristics:
- They are used to measure the progress made in identifying warriors in a community and supporting them as they pursue holistic wellness.
- They focus on access to earned benefits for veterans and the basic needs of housing and employment.
- They are measured across all organizations affiliated with America's Warrior Partnership and analyzed to identify local and national trends.
- They can be used to quantify the influence of earned veteran benefits in a community using America's Warrior Partnership's Index of Veteran Economic Impact©.

The first measurable objective relates to outreach and engagement. Without going out into the community and getting to know your warriors, the community services that exist, and the gaps in the services offered, your organization would be ineffective and unconnected. Outreach cannot be done behind a desk. It requires the staff to go out into the community and actively engage with its members. In the Community Integration model, outreach is the foundation upon which your veteran-centric nonprofit stands.

EXAMPLE GOAL 1: Make contact and establish a relationship with veterans living in your community.
EXAMPLE OBJECTIVE 1: Within the first three years of service to the community, your organization will make contact and establish relationships with a minimum of 80 percent of the post-9/11 warriors living in your community as estimated by the census data.

EXAMPLE GOAL 2: Increase the usage of the US Department of Veterans Affairs (VA) veteran education or training benefits and/ or vocational rehabilitation and employment programs within the population of known warriors.
EXAMPLE OBJECTIVE 2: Of the known warriors, 50 percent will utilize their post-9/11 GI Bill benefits as measured by the organization's collected data.

EXAMPLE GOAL 3: Increase the graduation rates of warriors enrolled in educational programs.
EXAMPLE OBJECTIVE 3: Of the known warriors enrolled in community education or vocational rehabilitation programs, 90 percent will graduate as measured by the organization's collected data.

EXAMPLE GOAL 4: Reduce the number of homeless warriors within the community.
EXAMPLE OBJECTIVE 4: Of the known warriors seeking housing, 70 percent will be housed as measured by the organization's collected data.

EXAMPLE GOAL 5: Reduce the unemployment rate within the population of known warriors.
EXAMPLE OBJECTIVE 5: Of the known warriors seeking employment who are employable, 94 percent (or 3 percentage points below the community average) will be employed as measured by the organization's collected data.

EXAMPLE GOAL 6: Enroll all known warriors in eBenefits.
EXAMPLE OBJECTIVE 6: Of the known warriors, 100 percent will be enrolled in eBenefits as measured by the organization's collected data.

EXAMPLE GOAL 7: Enroll all eligible known warriors in VA health care.
EXAMPLE OBJECTIVE 7: Of the known warriors, 100 percent of eligible warriors will be enrolled in VA health care as measured by the organization's collected data.

Community Integration Outcome

EXAMPLE OUTCOME: At the end of three years, 80 percent of known warriors within the community's catchment area will be actively engaged with the veteran-focused nonprofit. As a result, the Community Integration survey will report a 10 percent increase in the number of warriors indicating that they "feel more connected to the community."

Tracking Outcomes with a Customer Relationship Management Solution

Software is a necessity to effectively and efficiently track your organization's efforts and document its progress toward the achievement of its outcomes. The use of customer relationship management (CRM) software allows organizations to manage relationships, interactions, data, and information associated with warriors served.

A good CRM has the following characteristics:

- It is a case-coordination tool that enables the organization to stay connected to its clients, streamline processes, and improve effectiveness.

- It provides a secure location to collect pertinent warrior information, the warrior's individualized plan, the progress made by the warrior, and all interactions between the warrior and your organization.

- It provides your organization a place to document and assess its outcomes and produce reports on the data you have collected.

- Over time, it will help you discover trends and give you a better understanding of the veteran population that you serve.

Although you have the option to develop your own system, custom building a software solution has the following drawbacks:

- It takes time and money and may not be the best use of your resources.

- It has additional follow-on expenses associated with system maintenance, the cost and capability to connect with other platforms, and the ease of use for new employees or partners.
- It requires the assistance of someone technically savvy and experienced to design and develop a tool to meet your organization's needs.

Many of our community affiliates and partners use America's Warrior Partnership's privately managed application called WarriorServe®.

WarriorServe® has the following characteristics:

- It is built on the Salesforce® platform.
- It is a reliable, cost-effective, and secure solution.
- It simplifies data collection with warrior-specific customized fields and pick lists, thus reducing clerical errors.
- It streamlines the collection and analysis of critical warrior information, allowing communities to focus on providing holistic warrior care.
- It allows organizations to run reports at customizable intervals and visualize the data in their reports with dashboards.

More information about WarriorServe® is available from your designated America's Warrior Partnership support staff.

Fulfilling Obligations

Reporting on the common metrics established by America's Warrior Partnership ensures that your community remains compliant with your support agreement, but it also helps you maintain a strong focus on your mission to serve warriors holistically. Although the act of working with the veteran is the most important of duties, reporting on metrics is also a vital part of service delivery. Metrics allow you to show funders, grant providers, donors, and the community how you are using the money that you receive and the impact that it is having.

CHAPTER HIGHLIGHTS

 Outcomes are the results that come out of your organization's hard work and the keys to unlocking treasured funding sources.

 America's Warrior Partnership common Community Integration metrics were selected to support a holistic model of warrior support and represent concepts that resonate with healthy communities at large. Due to the diversity of communities, it is important to use standardized metrics to ensure an unbiased measure of community health and to quantify the successful outcomes of warrior-centric organizations.

 To verify outcomes and evaluate the results, you must first collect and then analyze the data. With today's cloud-based CRM software, data collection is simplified with customized fields and pick lists, reducing coding errors while saving you time.

 CRM technology provides your organization with the ability to track and analyze trends and patterns within your community, resulting in improved performance of your nonprofit and the ability to provide proactive support in your community.

CHAPTER 6:
LEVERAGING OUTCOMES

What's in this chapter?

✓ Tips and strategies for marketing and branding your organization
✓ Information about developing your marketing plan
✓ Strategies for utilizing media to tell your nonprofit's story
✓ Specific information about fundraising and development
✓ Tips and strategies for grant writing
✓ Tactics for implementing corporate and individual giving campaigns

"If you can't explain it simply, you don't understand it well enough."

~ Albert Einstein

TELLING YOUR STORY: BRANDING AND MARKETING

Nonprofits depend upon the goodwill of the communities in which they operate. This does not happen without effort. Successful nonprofits develop a plan that will do two things:
1. Bring the needs identified by the nonprofit to the attention of the community as well as the organization's efforts to address those needs.
2. Create easy access for the community to participate by giving, volunteering, or providing the nonprofit with in-kind donations.

Having a marketing plan that spells out what is needed, what is expected to be accomplished, and exactly how that will happen is essential to any nonprofit's success.

The Marketing Plan

The marketing plan needs to be developed by the nonprofit and must reflect its needs and activities.

The marketing plan should do the following:

- Address how to raise the profile of the organization and its mission within the community's consciousness.

- Expand to include new services when they are added to the nonprofit.

- Address the entire community but should be further tailored to each target audience based on the message and the action the organization hopes to ignite with each audience.

- Identify target audience members most likely to assist the nonprofit, and define what that assistance might look like.

- Encourage participation by local businesses that wish to reach veterans and service members. They might share advertising costs or hold joint events.

- Include a plan to cooperate with the local media on issues related to veterans and the military.

- Contain achievable goals, such as the following:
  - To double the nonprofit's followers on social media
  - To increase the number of public events held over the previous year
  - To participate in some new endeavor, such as sending out speakers to civic clubs
- Have a budget that can be used for such costs as printing materials for distribution, fees for vendor tables at events, or other necessary costs, including travel.
- Specify who on staff is responsible for carrying out the plan or certain parts of the plan. This might be a dedicated marketing person, or it might be the director of the nonprofit.

 TIP Should any parts of the plan be delegated to others, a clear line of reporting should be established.

Branding

Everything you do in public relations and media will face either the warrior population you hope to serve, the community you hope to work in, the supporters from whom you wish to receive funding and volunteer assistance, or some combination of any and all of these audiences.

When it comes to your organization's physical and digital presence, the old saying "you don't get a second chance to make a first impression" holds true; securing proper branding is of immense importance. Essentially, your organization's brand is its face, and of course, you want to put your best face forward from day one.

Your brand should
- reflect your organization's mission and core values;
- be professional; and
- be accurate and appealing.

Brand material includes the following:
- Logo
  - Select a symbol that truly embodies your organization's core values.

> **TIP** Find a clean design for digital and print purposes. When logos are too intricate, they tend to look pixelated and will not translate well across various platforms.

- Website and social media sites
  - These should reflect your brand guidelines.
  - These should highlight your mission statement.
- Business cards, letterhead, and marketing collateral.
  - These should reflect your brand guidelines.

Creating branding guidelines will help the staff in your organization consistently adhere to the branding principals.

Brand guidelines include the following:

- Cohesive color scheme
  - Primary—four or fewer main colors
  - Secondary—two alternative background colors
- Consistent font
  - Headline font
  - Body font
- Logo placement
  - Minimum size requirement
  - Border size constraints
  - Background colors
  - Includes information about how *not* to display the logo

Another essential part of branding is establishing your message platform and supporting key messages (talking points).

Consistent messaging is essential for several reasons:

- People generally need to see/hear a message multiple times before they remember it. To build brand awareness, your target audience needs to be able to understand what your organization does, which is achieved by being consistent with your messaging.
- It ensures that all people who represent your organization (senior leadership, board members, front desk staff, everyone!) are telling the same story and using the same messages when talking about

your organization. When folks are telling a different story, it leads to confusion and disengagement with an organization.

- Your key messages differentiate you from your competition and similar organizations in your space. Not only should your mission differ, but your key messages should reflect this differentiation.

When contemplating your message platform, ask yourself these questions:

- What does your organization represent?
- What work does it do?
- How does it do that work?

 ### Strategy for Creating your Message Platform and Key Messages

Message Platform

- Start with your mission statement and build on it by addressing the following elements: who, what, where, when, why, and how?
- The platform can be two to three sentences—it's better to keep it short. Save the extra detail for the supporting key messages.

Key Messages

- Bullet these out with detail. However, avoid adding excessive detail and making your message too complex.

EXAMPLE | *America's Warrior Partnership amplifies the efforts of veteran service organizations in communities across the country, providing resources and helping bridge gaps in services, so that those organizations can directly and more holistically support local veterans.*

TELLING YOUR STORY: SPREADING THE WORD

The measure of a successful nonprofit is not solely based on its ability to make a significant impact but also on its ability to tell its story. Your nonprofit may be able to track all sorts of metrics that illustrate your effectiveness to your stakeholders. But if you are not able to communicate this great work, your nonprofit will be unknown. To advance your mission, you must turn your data into a compelling story and communicate this story to your stakeholders and the funders. When broadcasting your story, it is vital to consider your audience when selecting your media platform.

Traditional media marketing is necessary for the audience that doesn't love all things online or doesn't consistently ingest digital marketing. Digital media is indispensable for those who do all transactions and many interactions online. So, a blend of traditional and digital media is necessary to get your story out.

General Notes on "Earned" Media

"Earned" media refers to anything that is not a paid placement—for example, working with a reporter as a source for a story he or she is writing.

When pursuing "earned" media, keep the following thoughts in mind:

- Relationships with earned media representatives (reporters, editors, producers, etc.) are key to receiving earned media.

- Identify the right media contacts who would cover the types of news or stories that could incorporate your organization. Reach out and begin to build a relationship—get to know their coverage needs, what interests them most, and so forth.

- Keep in mind that all media outlets are businesses trying to make money and serve the community.

- Be a good source: get your facts straight, don't expect miracles, be considerate of their time and needs, and be consistent.

- If they get something wrong, consider the impact of this before you create needless enemies. Was it a big mistake that could seriously hurt your organization's reputation, or was it a simple error?

> **TIP** Get and keep reporters on your side by going to them first with corrections and by going to their editors with praise for stories well done. Helpful reporters will fight to get your stories better play, whereas adverse ones can sink them.

Press Releases

Create press releases, simple announcements of news from your organization to the media, for all of your media outlets.

Good press releases have the following characteristics:

- Contain actual news, not feature story ideas
- Keep to a single page, with all contact information clearly stated
- Include who, what, where, when, why, and how of your news and mention if you have photos available
- Include the date sent at the top

Examples: news announcements, events, receipt of significant grant funding, recognition of your program by another source, awards, new hires on the executive level, or reorganization of your group

> Don't expect a press release to do the job of a public relations person. Press releases cannot develop community relationships and credibility like getting out into the community can.

Traditional Media

Each type of traditional media appeals to different audiences, has a unique value, and should be understood in the proper context. Although the influence of traditional media has shrunk in recent years due to the overwhelming shift to digital media, traditional media is still a well-respected news space and always should be considered, depending on the audience you are attempting to reach.

Types of traditional media include the following:

Print Media

- Newspapers and magazines still provide the bulk of local news coverage for any community.
- In most midsize communities, there is one local newspaper and maybe two or three niche papers that are published weekly or monthly. These niche papers often target specific populations,

such as youth, senior citizens, or ethnic groups, or are subject-matter specific. There may be an alternative newspaper that focuses on entertainment and more edgy topics.

- Print media are fact-focused, information-based outlets and may be approached without great art, although photos are always welcome.

- Print will frequently spill over into the digital realm because most newspapers manage websites as well.

 Strategies for Utilizing Newspapers and Magazines:
- Local newspaper
  – Find out if there is a reporter who covers the military and veteran issues.
  – Introduce yourself as a source for information about the reporter's beat, and give the reporter some story ideas.
  – Tell the reporter a success story. Describe changes that affect warriors.
  – Once you develop a relationship, the reporter will often come to you first whenever considering a story.

- Niche papers
  – Use these outlets as needed when your news affects their readership. There is no point in trying to sell an entertainment paper on a success story unless it ties into their readership. However, if one of your stories is that a famous rock group is backing your organization, go to that paper prepared for a cover story with great photos and access to the group for the article.

- Local magazine
  – Familiarize yourself with its contents and tailor your pitch to it.
  – Ask or find out the following:
    - Do they do monthly personality pieces, and if so, would your executive director fit there?
    - Has one of your warrior consumers accomplished something unique or overcome great obstacles?
    - Do you have great photos, or can they take some?

Television

- Television is a visual medium; don't expect a great story if no one is willing to get on camera.

- With TV, think: How can I best illustrate the story I am trying to tell? Showing a reporter or producer your ideas, with descriptive language, is going to be much more successful than making the reporter or producer figure out how to make it visual.

- Be mindful of their deadlines—TV works on very, very tight deadlines to produce multiple newscasts a day. Be open and forthcoming about this with TV personnel; ask their deadline, and ensure you can accommodate it.

- If you can't, just tell them—they will appreciate that more than you failing to deliver. But do so early so that they have time to fill the slot with another story.

- Keep in mind that TV advertising is not always the best use of your budget; it's costly and only exists in real time (that is, if viewers don't skip over your commercial using digital technology). It is important to weigh the cost and consider the audience before investing in this media.

Strategies for Utilizing Local Television

- If you have local stations, introduce yourself and your group to the highest-level people you can find. Tell them who you are and what you do. Don't wait for them to come to you.

- If you advertise, you might have greater access to the news side. Ask for some kind of discount, such as buy one, get one free, or additional space at another time.

- Call them whenever you are having an event, especially if it gives them an opportunity for great visuals.

- If there are morning or lunchtime interview programs, you can usually get on their schedule by merely asking.

Radio

Radio can be a great means to reach your audience because most people listen to the radio as they drive to and from work.

Strategies for Utilizing Local Radio Stations

- Find out if the local station offers a talk show on which you can appear.
  - Hone what you plan to say, whether in person or in a commercial.
  - If you have just fifteen seconds, make your point quickly and succinctly.

- Call stations and ask how to place a public service announcement (PSA).
  - These are simply unpaid commercials radio stations must run to satisfy the requirements of the Federal Communications Commission (FCC).
  - Find out the length needed and if you have to produce it yourself or if they will accept a written script.
  - These will likely be fifteen- to thirty-second spots, so again, pare your message down for this medium.

- Consider advertising for longer messages.

- If they have a news team, feed them stories appropriate for radio.

EXAMPLE | Include announcements of changes in benefits for veterans and information about job fairs, health events, concerts, and other events.

Outdoor

The main type of outdoor media is billboards.

- Although many billboards are still static, others are being replaced with digital ones that can, and do, change every few moments.

- Most often you will use billboards as part of an overall advertising package.

 TIP Outdoor advertising is often owned by other traditional media outlets, so you may be offered discounts if you also purchase advertising in the newspaper or radio station that controls it.

Digital Media

Welcome to the exciting and ever-changing world of digital media! You may be a multitasking digital media guru, just figuring out what hashtags are, or somewhere in between. No matter your personal usage, digital assets are ingrained in today's society to the point that we are completely "plugged in."

Being plugged in is not a bad thing by any means. It connects us and strengthens our relationships with loved ones, unites us with the world and like-minded individuals, and keeps us in the here and now. For businesses, the digital world is equally as important. Being in sync with digital technologies can dramatically increase your organization's recognition and appeal, forge strong two-way conversations between you and your constituents, and build unparalleled brand loyalty. This will ultimately make your organization thrive and rise to new heights. The best part is that most of these services are free or at least financially feasible.

Three Strategies for Digital Media Success

1. Build a solid digital foundation by learning, understanding, and appreciating the power of new technologies, platforms, and tools.

2. Know your target audience and their digital behaviors. To deliver information in the most compelling way possible, ask yourself:

   - What social media sites are used most often by my target audience?

   - Is my target audience more likely to share a social media post or an informative email?

3. Create a consistent distribution strategy. Keeping your content fresh and engaging is the key to standing out.

Website

A large part of your digital media presence is your website. Website design is critical, and not just for the visual appeal. Your website is more than a place to simply convey your organization's mission; your website is your organization's digital face. Naturally, you want to put your best face forward.

TIPS ❂ Think of your website as a candidate interviewing for a dream job. It should radiate professionalism and unwavering confidence.

❂ Your website should thoroughly and accurately answer any questions the audience may have.

Keeping your website streamlined and concise will supply your website's visitors with a superb user experience and create a memorable relationship. From the first design steps, you want to keep the user experience in mind. Make it easy to read and easy for people to interact with your organization, respond to your calls for action, and find the information they need to get assistance from your organization.

 TIP Strive to keep the most significant information "above the fold." This term originated with newspapers. They placed the most important information of the day on the front page, *above the fold*. In the world of web development, above the fold refers to the section of the website one initially sees before scrolling begins.

When developing a user-friendly website, it's important to incorporate the following components on your website's landing page:
- Logo
- Navigation bar
- Mission statement
- Easy access to the services you provide
- Visually enticing and relevant graphic(s)
- Call(s) to action
- Social media icons
- Subscription
- Easily visible contact information

To avoid a text-heavy website, distribute your content throughout different pages. These pages can be accessed from your website's navigation bar, which will be featured on every page.

Maintain a clean structure in your navigation bar by limiting the number of tabs to five or six main categories, with additional pages falling under these tabs as subitems.

The following tabs/pages should be included in your website:
- About Us
  - Our Mission
  - Staff
  - Board of Directors
- News
  - Pictures
  - Videos
- Get Involved
  - Donate
  - Volunteer
- Support Services
  - Service 1
  - Service 2
  - (and so forth as needed)

General Website Thoughts and Strategies

- Select a content management system (CMS) with innovative and straightforward site management capabilities that allow full control over your website. Example: WordPress is a CMS that allows you to populate and edit your site whenever you want, from wherever you want, without paying a web designer to do so.

- Use a complementary blend of compelling text and enticing media to showcase your organization's mission and work. Multidimensional content will leave a lasting impression on your audience.

- Make sure the information is accurate and to the point. You may lose the viewers' attention if your website is too text-heavy. State your message directly and clearly or risk not conveying it at all!

- Use a complementary blend of compelling text and enticing media to showcase your organization's mission and work. Multidimensional content will leave a lasting impression on your audience.

- Make sure the information is accurate and to the point. You may lose the viewers' attention if your website is too text-heavy. State your message directly and clearly or risk not conveying it at all!
- Keep the following ideas in mind when writing your web content:
  - Understand your audience. Keep their needs in mind, and create content they would want from your organization.
  - Format headlines properly.
  - Avoid "fluff"—keep your paragraphs relevant and concise.
  - Use terms that convey a call to action: "get involved," "learn more," "donate today."
  - Use proper grammar, spelling, and punctuation.
- Keep your website current and relevant.
  - Make a plan from the beginning to handle your content management in-house.
  - As your organization grows and changes, it is important that your website captures and shares these pivotal moments with your audience. Whether your organization has exciting news to share or if you are featured in the mainstream media, it needs to be available on your website as soon as possible.
- Use website analytics to monitor your website traffic. These tools allow you to see what pages, content, and campaigns visitors value most. You can then tailor your marketing plans to your exact audience and show potential sponsors or advertisers accurate and compelling data regarding who their audience will be.

EXAMPLE | Google Analytics tracks, monitors, and reports your website's traffic, demographics, acquisition (where the visitors originated from), consumer behaviors, and conversions (actions they took once on the site; i.e., made a donation). When you sign up for Google Analytics, you will be provided a tracking code and simple instructions on how to insert this

- Implement search engine optimization (SEO) to increase your chance of being recognized by search engines code into your website's code.

What is search engine optimization? In order to provide you accurate results when you perform a search on the internet, search engine "spiders" scan and filter out less relevant websites using complex algorithms. These algorithms measure a website's content, links, and keywords to decide if the website is relevant or not to your search. From a user's standpoint, the search engine filters are absolutely wonderful. However, when it comes to operating a website, navigating these algorithms can be tricky.

Keep in mind these basic SEO concepts:

- **Keywords** will help a search engine decipher if your organization's website matches a query. For example, to be found among the military population, your keyword may be "warrior." Place "warrior" in your website's title tag, page header, and content so that when the search engine crawls your website, it will deliver it to your target audience.

 Be careful with using too many keywords in your website's content because search engines view this as an illegitimate effort to garner attention.

- **Back-linking** is when another website lists your organization's link on their website as a virtual endorsement; the more outside websites link to yours, the higher your credibility is with search engines. Ask your partners to link to your website, and offer to link your website to theirs.

- **Site mapping** enables images on your website to be read by search engine spiders; in turn, this makes your ideas easier to find and gives your website higher rankings. A sitemap is the blueprint of your overall website, containing links to every page located throughout your site.

- **Blogs** on your website will instantly give you a higher SEO ranking. They allow you to quickly generate fresh content, which is a major factor in enhancing your SEO ranking, but also each post is viewed as an individual indexed page. This means the search engine spiders will spend more time on your site, gathering a variety of content that is beneficial to searchers.

Social Media

Another specific area of digital media that can significantly enhance your interaction with the community and the world is social media. It is one of the best promotional resources available to you as a nonprofit organization. Not only does it connect you with veterans, but it also connects you with their families, civilian supporters, and similar organizations on a national and global stage. The best part is, social media is a free and commanding asset.

To unleash the power of social media, you must abide by a few cardinal rules:

Rule 1: Have a solid strategy.
Contrary to popular belief, posting on social media is an art form that requires a well-planned strategy to avoid getting lost in the social media shuffle. To prevent this, you must know your target audience. If you are unsure who your audience is, go to your official Facebook business page and click on "See Insights." Like Google Analytics, Facebook Insights paints a clear picture of your audience ranging from demographical information to which type of posts your audience responds best to, even to what time of day they are most active on Facebook. All of this valuable information plays a pivotal part in making your posts stand out and go viral.

> **TIPS** ✪ Do not overpost! Posting two to three times a day is sufficient.
> ✪ Using the information from Facebook Insights, post when you know your audience is most active.
> ✪ Use hashtags to expand your reach and link to other pages when mentioning them in a post.

Rule 2: Create alluring content.
When creating content for social media, keep in mind that you want your content to reach as many people as possible.

Therefore, it is important to have a significant blend of text, photos, and videos to increase the probability of content sharing. To create alluring content:

- Highlight feature stories that would interest your audience.
- Create stories that feature people you serve.
- Produce in-house videos featuring staff members in order to form a more personal relationship with your target audience.
- Run contests.
- Share important news.
- Craft memes branded with your logo.
- Do research on similar organizations' social media pages. See what they are sharing, and find out what is getting the most engagement.

Rule 3: Get the conversation started!

Think of social media as a gateway to a dynamic conversation. Once your post is active, you can make a powerful connection with your target audience by interacting with them.

 TIPS ✪ When someone leaves you a comment, reply!

✪ Ask your audience a question. Not only will this build a relationship, but it will lay the foundation for a lasting one. When this happens, your posts have a better chance of being shared. We are social creatures by nature, and if you take the time to cultivate a relationship, it will prove to be a beneficial tactic that will enhance your organization's reputation.

FUNDING—GENERAL PHILOSOPHY AND CONCEPTS

Whether you are a new organization, a new program in an existing organization, a program started with the intention of being a spinoff organization, or a hybrid of public/private components, all organizations working on Community Integration are moving toward common goals:

- Expanding and improving services to warriors and their family members
- Becoming the community leader for warrior services
- Being a financially healthy, self-supporting organization

America's Warrior Partnership's overarching funding philosophy is that sustainable funding is within reach of all nonprofit organizations if they dedicate themselves to doing the work, sharing their results with people and organizations that have the means to support that work financially, and making them aware of both the organization's impact and need for financial support.

If you are a new organization, starting from the beginning, the nonprofit fundraising readiness information in the Development and Marketing section of the Toolkit will be helpful.

Funding—Fundraising and Development

Much focus in Community Integration is on the services offered to warriors, but we also want to help your organization become self-sustaining so that you can continue your services for the long haul. Our fundraising and development support is designed to ensure that your organization has a diversified funding mix to establish ongoing income and to provide protection if a single resource becomes unavailable.

The terms *fundraising* and *development* are often used synonymously. Although they are related, there are significant differences in the functionality of each.

Loren Anderson offers a useful description of the differences between fundraising and development in her article "'Fundraising' vs. 'Development': A Useful Distinction?":

Fundraising = Transactional

"Fundraising" describes an activity that is "transactional" in nature. The focus is on solicitation. An organization with a specific and short-term financial goal asks for a one-time, usually modest gift from a donor, usually for a specific cause or project.

Development = Relational

"Development," on the other hand, encourages us to think about our work in "relational" terms—the building, over time, of a continuous, powerful and life-long connection between a donor/philanthropist and the organization or cause we represent. When we approach our work as "development," the process includes extended cultivation, thorough education, and attentive stewardship—as well as appropriate solicitation!

Unlike fundraising, the development timetable is defined by the donor, the responses sought are multiple, and the goal is expansive—ultimately, a "lifetime" gift that permanently bonds the donor. Such gifts are life-changing, for our cause, and for the donor!

"Fundraising" and "development," of course, also work together. Every fundraising transaction is a signal to the perceptive development director, and it is, in many cases, the first step in building for the future.[12]

Fundraising and Fund Development

Your ability to fundraise and develop funding sources ties directly to meeting your annual budget needs. Most nonprofit organizations prefer to have a variety of funding sources and diversified funding streams to hedge against the inevitable changes that happen to funding ability over time.

Some common sources of funding that America's Warrior Partnership can help you explore include the following:

- Corporate contributions—Support from businesses whose key leaders understand your vision and may become involved as volunteers.

- In-kind support—Items and/or services donated instead of funds. Ideally, these are line items on your budget that are necessary to fulfill your mission.

---

[12]L. Anderson, "'Fundraising' vs. 'Development': A Useful Distinction?" last modified November 20, 2012, https://www.campbellcompany.com/news/bid/105288/Fundraising-vs-Development-A-Useful-Distinction.

- Individual donors—Monetary contributions from people who have been touched by your organization in some way.
- National and local foundations—Grants from organizations whose giving priorities align with the mission of your programs and/or services.
- Government grants and contracts—Federal, state, and local funds allocated to nonprofits to provide services to constituents.

There are countless ways to engage each of these groups in your fundraising and development plans.

Some engagement activities you may wish to consider are as follows:

- Special events—If you can sell a ticket to it, you can make it a fundraiser.
- Sponsorships—Provide businesses a way to "give back" while helping you create a financially successful event.
- Proposals—A letter appeal asking for specific support for a project or program. Proposals that match targeted funders' stated interest and mission to your project are more successful.
- Annual campaigns—An activity that occurs yearly to raise funds for operational expenses and to cultivate a donor base.
- Direct mail appeals—Directly appealing to your donor base with a well-written "ask" is more successful if it is part of a correspondence plan that includes thank-you notes, holiday cards, newsletters, and similar communications.

Because each nonprofit is unique and has access to different funding sources, there is no one-size-fits-all approach to fundraising.

To determine the best way to engage each funding source, you should consider the following:

- Assess your impact.
- Identify appropriate prospects.
- Devise a cultivation strategy before asking for support.
- Have a stewardship plan in place before asking for donations and applying for grants.

The development process can seem overwhelming when your primary focus is on serving veterans and helping to ensure their most basic needs are met. The Toolkit contains ideas and information to assist you with creating plans, tracking progress, tailoring your approach to different audiences, and building long-term relationships with donors and funders alike. Additionally, America's Warrior Partnership has dedicated team members to provide fundraising and development guidance and support.

Funding—Grants

The grant process is really about meeting needs, providing evidence of results obtained, and becoming partners. Grantmakers have goals and objectives they want to reach through their funding. Grant receivers have goals and objectives they want to achieve with the support they are given. The ideal situation is when a grant maker and a grant receiver have very similar goals and can work together to reach them.

> **TIP** If you learn that your organization's mission and focus does not match with a particular funder, you should not waste time pursuing a grant that will most likely not be funded.

To ensure success, you should consider these three factors from the very beginning when writing the grant proposal:
1. The person writing the grant proposal should be very knowledgeable about the capabilities of the organization and its collaborating partners. This person should consider the staff and resources the organization already has available internally and externally and the cost associated with using those resources.
2. The grant writer should do research to determine the cost for additional resources if they will be needed in the future to achieve grant requirements.
3. The grant writer should be aware of the programs the organization offers and the time it will take for each program to achieve required goals and objectives.

If the grant proposal considers the organization's capabilities and how it will meet time, scope, and budget requirements, grant management will be a much smoother process.

Rules for grant writing:

1. *Follow the instructions!* Be complete with narratives and attachments. Assemble it in the manner the funder requests. Turn it in on time (or early). Ask questions if the instructions are not clear.

2. Focus on effective communication and concise writing, and tell the stories of people whose lives are touched by your work. Be clear and edit your work mercilessly.

3. Pay close attention to reporting requirements. Being honest and transparent builds trust between a funder and a program.

Ways to identify available grant funding opportunities:

- Research opportunities using the internet and internet-accessible databases.

- Write letters of inquiry to funders.

- Obtain grant applications from funders that have open or unrestricted funding opportunities.

Grant application strategies:

- It is imperative that you develop a grants calendar to track deadlines for applications, reports, attachments, and so forth.

- Always plan backward from the deadlines to ensure you have enough time for your work and the assistance you need from others (finance, program, board approval, etc.) before the deadline.

- Never wait until the last minute to submit an application. You never know when something will go wrong.

- Do not assume that things are the same from year to year. Some grantors have been known to change their application form each year to trip up those who are on autopilot.

- Be sure that you can provide appropriate measurable outcomes for your program objectives, not just outputs. Sometimes outputs are desirable as part of the way you show your work, but many funders want to see what effect your work is having, along with an account of the work you are doing.

Detailed information on each part of the grant-writing process is included in the Development and Marketing section of the Toolkit.

Grant Compliance and Stewardship

Grant recipients are responsible for managing grant funds in compliance with statutes, rules, grant agreements, agency policies, and other applicable laws and requirements. With this list of responsibilities, it is easy to recognize the pivotal part grant management plays in the success of a nonprofit's program.

 Strategies for grant management:

- Establishing a single point of contact for grantee-to-grantor communication helps establish a trusting relationship with the grantor and makes grant management more efficient. This job can be a full-time position if your funding portfolio consists of many grants or a part-time role if your volume of grant funding is low.

- There are three equally important aspects agreed upon in the grant proposal and award letter/agreement that must be managed:
  1. Time (e.g., meeting reporting, task, and expenditure deadlines)
  2. Scope (e.g., meeting goals and objectives)
  3. Budget (e.g., spending funds appropriately)

Having a firm grasp on where grant funds are being spent and meeting deadlines is just as important as meeting goals and objectives.

- Create a grant management plan to set your organization up for success and to ensure everyone is focused on grant compliance. This grant plan should map out how the organization is going to stay on time to meet goals and objectives and stay on budget.

The budget part of the grant plan should include the following:
- A description of acceptable expenses as well as unacceptable expenses
- Dates for periodic meetings to review the budget versus actual expenses so that the organization can determine if it is on track with spending
- A plan for proper communication to ensure accounting staff and spending-approval managers are aware of the budget, approved expenses, and the status of spending and can monitor for overspending or underspending

The plan to meet goals and objectives should include the following:
- A list of resources, both internal and external, that will be used during the grant period to help achieve the goals and objectives
- A description of how to properly measure the goals and objectives
- A breakdown of tasks necessary to complete in order to meet those goals and objectives, as well as a deadline for each task
- A breakdown of each task, measurement of success, and deadlines for internal and external staff members
- A plan for regular meetings during the grant period for the entire team doing the work to check in on progress toward meeting the goals and objectives

Failure to properly manage grants can be detrimental to the organization's reputation and funding stream. If you don't comply with a grant's requirements, there can be real—and damaging—consequences. It can result in a loss of current grant funding as well as put you at risk of being denied for future grants. News travels fast among community funders. Maintaining grant compliance is imperative.

Corporate Giving

According to Giving USA 2017, corporate giving represents only 5 percent of total charitable giving. However, the $18.55 billion corporations give annually is a large enough chunk of money to make chasing corporate giving worthy of your organization's efforts.[13] Additionally, the recent trend in corporate social responsibility could also benefit your organization. The Community Integration model that empowers communities to empower warriors seems like a natural fit for corporations seeking to improve the quality of life in the communities where they operate.

In the article "4 Smart Ways Nonprofits Can Tap into Corporate Giving," Elizabeth Chung offers some great advice for seeking corporate funding:

- Choose a local partner that is like-minded in mission and congruent in size.

- When approaching the potential partner, be prepared to describe the value (regarding community impact and publicity) that a partnership with your organization brings to them.

- Ask the partner to consider sponsoring a donation match campaign. This helps corporations increase their donation's community impact and gain wider positive publicity.

- At the beginning of your partnership, consider asking your corporate partners to provide in-kind support. This donation of goods or staff expertise satisfies their corporate social responsibility and engages their employees in the corporation's philanthropic mission.[14]

Individual Giving

According to Giving USA 2017 statistics, donations from individuals, ordinary people like you and me, provide 80 percent of the private funding that supports nonprofits.[15] Ironically, the fundraising efforts for many nonprofits focus mostly on seeking donations from corporations and foundations rather than individuals. Although companies and foundations generally give to help a project or

---

[13]Giving USA, "See the Numbers—Giving USA 2017 Infographic," last modified June 12, 2017, https://givingusa.org/see-the-numbers-giving-usa-2017-infographic/.

[14]E. Chung, "4 Smart Ways Nonprofits Can Tap into Corporate Giving," accessed March 29, 2018, https://www.classy.org/blog/4-smart-ways-nonprofits-can-tap-into-corporate- giving/.

[15]Giving USA, "See the Numbers—Giving USA 2017 Infographic," last modified June 12, 2017, https://givingusa.org/see-the-numbers-giving-usa-2017-infographic/.

organization advance from one stage to the next, individuals generally give to support an organization's long-term success.

Knowing that 80 percent of nonprofit funding comes from individual donations should be enough to pique interest, but there are several other reasons why a nonprofit should focus on its individual donors. In the article "Making the Case for Individual Giving," Maureen Mahoney Hill (2015) offers a few reasons why you should consider creating an individual giving campaign:

- Unlike corporate and foundation donations that are earmarked for a particular purpose or project, individual giving is unrestricted (unless specifically restricted by the donor). Unrestricted funds can go toward any purpose, including operating expenses.
- Fundraising sustainability is fortified by effective individual giving campaigns. Individuals tend to become loyal funders who donate annually and often increase their contributions year over year.
- Often, this loyal fund base can be a source to tap into for volunteers.
- If properly tended, planned gifts can result from individual giving.[16]

Types of individual giving initiatives:
- Annual campaigns
- Special events
- Direct mail appeals

The Fundraising Cycle

Fundraising involves more than crafting a cute email asking individuals for a donation. Understanding the fundraising cycle can move your fundraising efforts from acceptable to successful. The article "How to Create an Individual Giving Program" by Amy Eisenstein identifies the following four steps to crafting a successful

---

[16]M. M. Hill, "Making the Case for Individual Giving," last modified February 26, 2015, https://nonprofittalent.com/making-the-case-for-individual-giving/.

individual giving strategy:

Step 1: Identify Prospects

- Look to your past donors for prospects.
- Ask your board and staff for names of friends or business contacts that might identify with your mission.
- Identify approximately twenty of your best potential donors for each fundraising event.

Step 2: Cultivate

- Start cultivating a relationship with the best potential donors.
- Tell them about your organization and learn more about them.
- Bring potential donors into your organization to see how your organization empowers veterans by connecting them to community service providers.
- Invite potential donors to events that your organization is holding.

Step 3: Solicit

- Now that you have established a relationship with the prospective donors, they know about your organization, and you know about them, it's time to ask for a donation.
- It is wise to first ask for a reasonable annual donation for a specified amount targeted for an identified purpose.
- Once you have asked, stay quiet and give the potential donors a few minutes to respond. If they offer a donation, find out how they want to provide it. If they don't desire to donate at this time, don't be discouraged. Try to find out if it just an issue with the amount or the project. Sometimes "no" just means "not now."

Step 4: Steward

- Now that you have donors, it's important you turn them into loyal donors by appreciating their gifts.
- Thanking a donor is the best way to keep a donor. There are many ways to say thanks; cards, emails, newsletters, public appreciation, and personal thank-you statements are among the various ways to say thank you for a donation.[17]

---

[17]A. Eisenstein, "How to Create an Individual Giving Program," last modified March 11, 2015, http://www.amyeisenstein.com/how-to-create-an-individual-giving-program/.

America's Warrior Partnership's
Annual #IAMAWARRIOR Campaign

As an affiliate organization, you are eligible to participate in America's Warrior Partnership's annual campaign, #IAMAWARRIOR. Participating in this campaign builds individual contributions while igniting awareness and support.

- The campaign kicks off each November and continues through the end of the year.

- The prep will be done for you, including creating the landing page, social media toolkit, sample emails, and graphics.

- All you need to do is create a team page and promote it in a big way. It's a peer-to-peer campaign where you will be able to add as many team members (fundraisers) to your team as you like. Publicize it through social media, emails, and other connections.

- At the end of the campaign, we will send you a check for the contributions your team raises, minus the Classy.org and PayPal fees that we must pay.

Additional tools and techniques you can use to raise money from individuals can be found in the Development and Marketing section of the Toolkit.

CHAPTER HIGHLIGHTS

- Having a marketing plan that spells out what is needed, what is expected to be accomplished, and exactly how that will happen is essential to any nonprofit's success.

- To advance your mission, you must turn your data into a compelling story and communicate this story to your stakeholders and funders.

- Sustainable funding is within reach of all nonprofit organizations if they dedicate themselves to doing the work, sharing their results with people and organizations that have the means to support that work financially, and making them aware of both the organization's impact and need for financial support.

- America's Warrior Partnership has dedicated team members who can provide guidance and support for fundraising and development.

CHAPTER 7:
MAINTAINING A PROGRAM

What's in this chapter?

✓ Information about assessing and evaluating your veteran- focused nonprofit program

✓ Examples of internal and external assessments for evaluating a nonprofit following the Community Integration model

✓ Strategies to multiply your outcomes

✓ Specific program evaluation tips from America's Warrior Partnership

"Coming together is a beginning; keeping together is progress; working together is success."

~ Henry Ford

ASSESSMENT AND EVALUATION OVERVIEW

At this point, we have discussed how to build your program, how to measure your program, and how to leverage your program's success. Improving your Community Integration program through proper assessment and evaluation is the next vital building block to achieving successful outcomes.

To grow and improve a Community Integration program, you must participate in regular evaluations.

Evaluations have the following characteristics:
- They encourage you to be proactive as opposed to reactive.
- They are essential to maintaining quality service.
- They improve program sustainability.
- They help maintain transparency.

Evaluations should be performed through both internal and external assessments.

Internal assessments:
- Allow you to identify on-the-spot ways to improve your services to veterans and their families/caregivers
- Are cost-effective and provide quick results
- Increase your success rate in achieving outcomes and staying on track with goals, if conducted regularly

Internal evaluations specific to Community Integration include the following:
- Reviewing dashboards and reports
- Performing internal audits
- Reviewing and revising a program development plan
- Completing a regular self-assessment of services
- Measuring community impact
- Maintaining strong finances by reviewing and updating your budget

External assessments:

- Can provide you with out-of-the-box ways to think about your program and the services you offer
- Can provide evidence to establish the credibility of your program
- Are more expensive because they are conducted by people outside your organization
- Are impactful because they are completed by a nonbiased party
- Show your organization's willingness to be transparent

External evaluations specific to Community Integration include the following:
- Obtaining feedback from customers
- Obtaining feedback from partners
- Participating in a third-party program audit conducted by America's Warrior Partnership

EVALUATION OF PROGRAM SERVICES

Offering quality service is the most crucial factor in implementing the Community Integration model and in maintaining your nonprofit's reputation. As they say in business, it is three times more expensive to find a new customer than it is to retain a current customer. This is also true for nonprofits. As we discussed in chapter 1, if you do the work, the funding will come. However, this only is true if the work is proven to be done well. Services can be evaluated internally as well as externally to ensure your work is meeting expectations.

Internal Evaluations

- Reports are useful tools for internally evaluating the quality of your services.

    Aspects of monthly reports include the following:
    - They can be effortlessly pulled from your customer relationship management (CRM) system.
    - They should be reviewed by the program manager.

– They can help you determine if you are achieving your target outcomes. If a number is falling short, you may need to reallocate resources or explore new partnerships to assist in providing services.

These reports can be utilized to create a picture of your data. Some CRMs will generate dashboards that are a graphic representation of your data. Dashboards are useful tools to help you visualize a snapshot in time of your program's operations. You can create custom dashboards for each employee based on the figures the employee wants or needs to see.

Dashboards have the following benefits:

– They help managers distribute work and prioritize tasks for employees.

EXAMPLE | A useful dashboard for a program manager would be one that shows the amount of time it takes for a veteran to receive services/support. This allows the manager to monitor a team's ability to deliver services to veterans within a reasonable time.

– They help employees work more efficiently.

EXAMPLE | A useful dashboard for a case coordinator would be one that shows the total number of open cases. This gives the case coordinator a quick reference on which cases to prioritize for the day.

• Internal program audits are also helpful to evaluate your services. Internal audits are observational evaluations that help identify if employees are following quality standards. If a standard is consistently not being observed, it is important to analyze whether or not the standard is necessary. If it is, then a program must identify ways to enforce the rule. If it is not, the program should eliminate the practice to avoid wasting time and resources or slowing down progress. To safeguard the quality of service, consider auditing your internal controls.

The internal controls most often examined are the following:

– Documentation and procedures for proper communication and record retention
– Process and procedures for tracking of services
– Procedures for monitoring grants and contract compliance
– Validation of accurate and reliable financial reporting

You can create your own internal program audit based on the quality measures you would like to maintain, or you can consult with a company to craft quality measures for you. However, the cost of consultation with an external source can be expensive. If you participate in an external audit on an annual basis, you may be able to use the audit information to build an internal audit procedure.

 TIPS America's Warrior Partnership recommends that internal audits should not be performed more than quarterly. Quarterly audits provide staff with enough time to adjust their practices based on the audit findings.

External Evaluations

• Third-party external audits provide an unbiased view of your Community Integration program to assess sustainability, effectiveness, and areas for improvement.

• America's Warrior Partnership's Annual Comprehensive Audit

– Provides affiliates with an evaluation of their services

– Provides recommendations for service improvement; the areas evaluated are as follows:
  :: Program progress
  :: Overall management systems/structure
  :: Outreach and targeting (marketing)
  :: Consumer eligibility
  :: Case coordination of supportive services
  :: Financial management
  :: Policies and procedures

- Surveys provide an effective means for external evaluation. It is essential to ask veterans and family members/caregivers to give feedback on the services they receive.
  - Veteran surveys developed by your organization are important external assessments for the following reasons:
    :: Ultimately, your reason for existence is to serve veterans.
    :: All feedback is good feedback. If you receive an unsatisfactory evaluation from a customer, it should be analyzed. A program should consider if this is an individual issue or a program issue. If the problem is an individual issue, pocket the information to ensure the problems don't persist. If the issue is a program issue, take proper measures to solve the problem.
    :: A nonprofit is only as good as the services it provides to the community.
  - America's Warrior Partnership's Annual Warrior Survey
    :: Provides affiliates with veteran feedback and information about current trends in their community
    :: This survey has the following characteristics:
      - Is anonymous, which allows participants the ability to speak their mind freely
      - Asks veterans questions about the services they would like to receive
      - Asks veterans if they feel the services provided are helping
      - Asks veterans how satisfied they are with the services

Knowing how veterans feel about the services your organization provides helps your nonprofit grow stronger and better meet the needs of the community.

Evaluating Your Nonprofit's Partner Interactions

The objectives of the Community Integration model are not only to maintain quality service to veterans and their family members/caregivers but also to ensure the veteran-focused nonprofits are making case coordination a positive experience for their partners. The Community Integration program is only as robust as the resources available. Therefore, it is essential to check in regularly with your partners.

Useful methods of assessing your interactions are as follows:
- Analyzing reports
- Asking questions
- Making personal observations

EXAMPLES — If a partner has a delayed response when it receives a referral, it may be a sign that the partner has a high case volume. It would be worth a phone call to check in with the partner to ask how things are going. Not looking for the root of the problem can reflect poorly on your program and slow down services to veterans.

— If referrals to your program have slowed down from a partner, it may be a sign the partner is not satisfied with your service. It is important to regularly communicate with your partners to maintain healthy relationships and ensure veterans are receiving the resources they need.

Program Sustainability

Continuous evaluation of your services is essential, not only to improve support for veterans and their families/caregivers but also to ensure program sustainability. If your nonprofit's plan is to serve the community for years to come, then sustainability needs to be a well-thought-out aspect of the program. A program development plan (PDP) can help you ensure program sustainability by helping you stay on track with your action plan.

Characteristics of and guidelines for PDPs are as follows:
- It is a tool to evaluate your operational performance.
- It should be created at the beginning of your program implementation process and reviewed on a monthly basis.
- It should include the following:
  - A list of goals
  - Program findings, including triumphs, changes, and issues
  - An action plan for staying on track to achieve program goals

- It should include an annually updated strategic plan section that contains the following:
  - An outreach plan
  - A program plan
  - A financial plan
  - A marketing plan
    :: The marketing plan should include a SWOT analysis. A brainstorm session is a good practice to help you identify several items for each section.

SWOT is an analysis of the internal and external factors that affect the success of your program. SWOT stands for strengths, weaknesses, opportunities, and threats. When performing a SWOT analysis, it is important to recognize that strengths and weaknesses are internal factors that affect the program, whereas opportunities and threats are external factors that affect the program.

EXAMPLE | SWOT:
- **S**trengths: Dedicated staff
- **W**eaknesses: Limited funding
- **O**pportunities: Strong partnerships
- **T**hreats: Anticipated economic downturn

CHAPTER HIGHLIGHTS

 To grow and improve a Community Integration program, you must participate in regular evaluations.

 Evaluations should be performed through both internal and external assessments.

 The Community Integration program is only as robust as the resources available. Therefore, it is essential to check in regularly with your partners.

 A program development plan can help you stay on track to achieve your program goals.

CHAPTER 8:
ADDITIONAL BEST
PRACTICES FOR SUCCESS

What's in this chapter?

✓ Additional information and concepts vital for successful implementation of the Community Integration model

"Ultimately, leadership is not about glorious crowning acts. It's about keeping your team focused on a goal and motivated to do their best to achieve it, especially when the stakes are high, and the consequences really matter. It is about laying the groundwork for others' success, and then standing back and letting them shine."

~ Retired Col. Chris Hadfield,
Canadian Astronaut

Ethics and Confidentiality in Service

As a community leader in social services, many people have high expectations for how you will conduct your service and business. A list of best practices related to ethics and confidentiality is offered here to guide you. The National Association of Social Workers (NASW) Code of Ethics[18] informs much of this information.

- A warrior's best interest and well-being must be the case coordinator's primary concern. In some states, mandatory reporting laws obligate case coordinators to report situations in which a warrior threatens harm to self or others. Following the regulations is always in the best interest of both parties. It is a good idea to verify your state's requirements for mandatory reporting laws.

- Warriors must be allowed self-determination. Their wisdom or experience may be different from yours, but that does not make it less valuable or less correct. You must strive to prioritize their values, their dreams, and their way of doing things over your personal thoughts or solutions.

- You are ethically bound to protect the confidentiality of the warriors you serve. A warrior must give informed consent to participate in your services. Written permission must be obtained before disclosing personal and case-related information. Each warrior should have knowledge and understanding of what he or she is consenting to in receiving services, including sharing of information as needed for effective and efficient case coordination. (You can find an example consumer authorization form in the Toolkit.)

- Protecting the privacy of warriors' personal and case information extends to protecting the security of records in paper and electronic forms.

- Your organization's confidentiality policies should detail the cases in which disclosure can be made without consent, such as in cases of a legal obligation or obligation to prevent imminent harm.

---

[18]National Association of Social Workers, "Code of Ethics," last modified 2017, https://www. socialworkers.org/About/Ethics/Code-of-Ethics/Code-of-Ethics- English.

- Be sure your organization has a policy about sharing (or not sharing) information when multiple family/household members are receiving assistance. If you are working with a warrior who lacks decision-making capacity, it is incumbent upon the case coordinator to safeguard the best interests and rights of the warrior. In this situation, you should work to obtain appropriate assistance for the warrior and/or work on the warrior's behalf with a caregiver or family member.

- You should also have a policy about warrior privacy and the media so that those you are serving are aware of how you may use their stories or likenesses for the purposes of publicity, fundraising, increasing awareness, or advocacy.

- All staff should be trained in the protection of privacy and confidentiality and should be vigilant about how and where discussion of cases occurs.

- If your organization is required to be compliant with the Health Insurance Portability and Accountability Act (HIPAA), many other things apply, and you will need a notice of privacy practices (NOPP) and other documents in your intake packet to satisfy those requirements. A sample NOPP is provided in the Toolkit.

- You must be competent. Do not attempt to do work for which you are not qualified and/or trained. Refer warriors to other resources for assistance or services that are outside your capability or training.

- Always be informed by cultural competence. Cultural awareness is a learned skill. Be aware of your own cultural identity and views about cultures different from yours. Training is available to help you learn to effectively interact with people who come from a different cultural background than you. (For more information, see the "Military Culture" and "Multicultural Competence" sections later in this chapter.)

- Avoid conflicts of interest. It is best to refrain from mixing personal and professional lives. If this cannot be avoided, you should take steps to inform all involved parties of your conflict of interest and to limit the impact the conflict has on the organization and its business. This could apply to employees, contractors, volunteers, or board members who receive a financial advantage from their relationship with your organization. It could also involve any of those groups sharing knowledge about your organization's internal workings with other groups or organizations or drawing benefit to another agency where they may concurrently sit on the board or are employed. Conflicts can also arise when a family or household member of an employee, contractor, volunteer, or board member gains a financial or other advantage through the connection to your organization.

- Your position as a helping organization inherently puts every employee, intern, volunteer, and representative of your organization in a position of power in relation to the warriors you serve. This applies to current, former, and future warrior consumer relationships as well as the relatives or close personal friends of the warrior and the person in power. Even if you would be a peer or equal to this individual in another setting, the act of receiving assistance from your organization means that the warrior is in a power-imbalance situation. You should avoid physical contact, harassment of any kind, romantic or sexual relationships, any misuse or abuse of power, and inappropriate gifts. Your organization should define what gifts are appropriate versus inappropriate. (Refer to the "Professional Boundaries" section later in this chapter for more information.)

- You must exemplify trustworthiness. You should operate with integrity, tell the truth, and be reliable in your dealings with warriors and colleagues.

- You should strive to treat people equally and avoid favoritism. You must be self-aware and check for tendencies to provide a different level of service or help for warriors whom you may find to be difficult to work with, who are unlike you, or who are not making the decisions you would make.

Military Culture

Military culture can be very different from civilian culture, and those who come from either background may not be aware of the differences or the degree to which a person's worldview is influenced by his or her personal, cultural experience. These differences can often create barriers and lead to misunderstandings.

One of the most significant barriers to warriors seeking services or assistance can be that they are unfamiliar with the role of asking for help or assistance due to the following reasons:

- They are accustomed to offering service and being the helper, rather than receiving help.
- Military service members are trained to be confident, to overcome challenges, to find a way to surmount obstacles, and to maintain focus on the goal they are given.

Upon leaving military service, warriors who are accustomed to having decisions curated or made for them are faced with a civilian world in which they now must choose for themselves from a myriad of opportunities and organizations for services. This can be an overwhelming experience that creates significant stress.

Due to the transient nature of military-affiliated life, it is standard operating procedure for warrior households to have much of their lives laid out for them in a strip-map format. When civilians move for a job, they usually hire their own moving company, find their own home in a new community, and may have few connections in their new town to introduce them to stores, service providers, and community amenities. By contrast, when a military household moves to a new duty station, the moving process is structured by the base transportation office. Housing may be in government quarters, and a family center at the new duty location can provide information for on-post and off-post options for shopping, medical services, child care, and recreation. When a warrior is deployed in a combat zone, the experience is even more intense and focused.

Advocates who understand how military culture can affect the decisions and experiences of its members will be able to individualize care. It is imperative that workers and organizations be familiar with the practices and beliefs of the military culture so that they can deliver culturally appropriate services.

To improve their military cultural awareness, case coordinators/advocates should do the following:

- Have and continue to develop specialized knowledge and understanding about military history, traditions, values, and systems as they relate to warriors.

- Understand that warriors are influenced by their professional cultures, such as the characteristics of the branch of the uniformed services in which they serve, their primary duty military occupation, and their combat status.

- Be able to identify and resolve biases, myths, and stereotypes about military culture and how this culture integrates into civilian life.

- Recognize the possibility of discrimination or prejudice toward warriors based on their military service and understand that it can have the same effect as other forms of bias and prejudice.

For more information, see the following resource links:

"Advanced Social Work Practice in Military Social Work," a 2010 publication of the Council on Social Work Education, available at www.cswe.org/CMSPages/GetFile.aspx?guid=75fa605c-03ff-44fb-a6f8-57d102e6fde5

America's Warrior Partnership's online training site, which contains military culture competence training created by PsychArmor, available at http://americaswarriorpartner.litmos.com .

Multicultural Competence

The warriors with whom we work come from a variety of backgrounds and contexts. As helping professionals, it is essential to work from a place of multicultural competence. This means that staff members must consider both the racial and ethnic diversities of the warrior, further taking into consideration the warrior's sexual orientation, spirituality, ability and any disabilities, and social class and economics, as well as the potential for any cultural bias by the practitioner.

Multicultural competence can be demonstrated by your organization in the following ways:

- Staff members should have knowledge of, and respect for, cultures that differ from their own. Information about cultures that are common among those you serve should be addressed in staff training. You should also train staff in appropriate ways to work with and learn from warriors who come from cultural backgrounds with which the staff is unfamiliar.

- Staff should develop habits of self-awareness so that they can recognize their own potential for bias and create coping strategies to keep their prejudices from influencing the service they provide to warriors.

- Your organization should reflect the cultures represented in your service population within its staff, volunteers, and leadership. This cultural reflection will result in a robust team that is not too biased or focused in one cultural context.

- Include training opportunities and awareness for your interns, volunteers, board members, and administrative or leadership staff.

Creating a safe place for people from all backgrounds will show that your organization is worthy of the trust you are asking the community to put in you as the leader in warrior/veteran outreach and engagement. For training on multicultural competency, consider utilizing the free online course available at www.train.org/vha/course/1062987.

Risk Mitigation/Liability

Many organizations think about liability issues as the things that need to be approved by a lawyer. It is both responsible and vital to have legal consultation available to protect your staff, your volunteers, and your organization. The following are practices that will help limit your exposure to situations that could create headaches and distract from your primary goals to coordinate support for warriors and provide community leadership for warrior concerns:

- Do not assume that consumers, community members, or other organizations have your organization's best interests as their top priority. Even if your organization is committed to operating transparently and truthfully with others, do not assume that everyone else is doing the same. Sooner or later, you will encounter a partner that does not share your values. Think about how you will handle this challenge before it occurs so that you are prepared to maintain your integrity in the moment of trial.

- Be careful with whom you align your organization—do your due diligence for both organizations and individuals. Use your networks to inquire about the way potential partners have worked with others in the past. Check provided references as well as those who know about a person or agency but are not voluntarily given as a reference—alternate sources could confirm what you have already heard or provide a different viewpoint. Be sure to follow hiring and human resources laws when you are researching potential employees.

- Pay attention to common areas where liability could arise: driving, the physical setting of your workspaces (slip, trip, and fall; general safety; American with Disabilities Act [ADA] compliance), handling money, handling the personal information of consumers or donors.

- Train staff and volunteers in ways to limit liability, and have them sign an acknowledgment form for their personnel files covering the areas of training.

- Be sure your hiring practices include motor vehicle records, background checks, and/or credit checks for appropriate jobs. If your insurance company requires or recommends it, implement preemployment and other screening for alcohol and substance use.

- Pay attention to the compliance requirements of grantors—their conditions are not always directly related to the thing you have received their funding to do.

- Have a lawyer available for free or low-cost consultation for liability concerns and questions.

Employee Sustainability: Reducing Compassion Fatigue and Burnout

Working in a helping profession can be mentally and emotionally challenging. High levels of stress take a toll on the work productivity and personal lives of many people working in social services.

In the article "Coping with Caring: The Dangers of Chronic Stress and Burnout," Kristin Duare McKinnon wrote the following:

> I define stress as the experience of discomfort, which can be emotional, physical, mental, or a combination of all three. This discomfort is caused by our inability to meet certain demands or expectations in our lives, which in turn leaves us feeling threatened, inadequate and vulnerable.

> Stress can be external—caused by a change or the lack of control—or internal—based on our perceptions and expectations. Feeling stress is our mind and body's unique way of letting us know that something is wrong and that we need to make changes to feel good again. Unfortunately, we often ignore these warning signs and learn to adapt to a stressful lifestyle instead of taking steps to reduce and control our stress. The danger of ignoring stress is that it can become chronic—negatively affecting all facets of our lives. Experiencing chronic stress over long periods of time can lead us to the mental, physical and emotional exhaustion known as burnout. Burnout, which happens when our minds and bodies simply cannot continue to function under the stress of our lives, can lead to serious emotional or physical illness, disability or even death.[19]

Tips for fighting burnout include the following:

- Reaching out for support from colleagues or friends
- Seeking a new perspective on the most troublesome issues at hand
- Taking a physical or mental rest by changing your activity

---

[19]K. Duare McKinnon, "Coping with Caring: The Dangers of Chronic Stress and Burnout," last modified July 6, 1996, https://beta.charityvillage.com/cms/content/topic/coping_with_caring_the_ dangers_of_ chronic_stress_and_burnout#.WgtW8Ibas3g).

- Sticking to boundaries related to work
- Maintaining healthy eating habits and regular physical activity
- Sharing coping strategies with others

Tips for helping fellow team members reduce stress include the following:

- If you see a coworker struggling with stress, reach out and acknowledge the person's stress and listen. Many times, simply saying, "Are you OK? You seem a bit stressed," will start the ball rolling. Allowing a person to vent will release some frustration.
- Encourage your stressed-out coworker to take a break and go for a walk with you. Sometimes just the act of leaving the office and going outside can help relieve stress.

Tips for leaders to reduce employee stress include the following:[20]

- Set clear expectations and goals.
- Make sure the workloads are realistic.
- Communicate by offering feedback, listening to ideas, and keeping employees updated on changes and plans.
- Encourage a healthy work–life balance.
- Allow for flexible work schedules and remote work when possible.
- Encourage breaks, physical exercise, and relaxation training.

A research-based discussion of the positive and negative mental aspects of helping others can be found on the Professional Quality of Life website (www.proqol.org), which notes the following:

Professional quality of life is the quality one feels in relation to their work as a helper. Both the positive and negative aspects of doing your work influence your professional quality of life. People who work helping others may respond to individual, community, national, and even international crises. They may be healthcare professionals, social service workers, teachers, attorneys,

---

[20]C. Mendex, "How to Reduce Stress among Employees at a Nonprofit," accessed March 15, 2018, http://www.firstnonprofitcompanies.com/how-to-reduce-stress-among- employees-at-a-nonprofit/.

police officers, firefighters, clergy, transportation staff, disaster responders, and others. Understanding the positive and negative aspects of helping those who experience trauma and suffering can improve your ability to help them and your ability to keep your own balance.[21]

This website offers many useful, free resources, including a manual, a self-scoring Compassion Satisfaction and Compassion Fatigue inventory, and a quick reference card for service providers.

America's Warrior Partnership's online training site contains veteran employee sustainability competence training created by PsychArmor (http://americaswarriorpartner.litmos.com).

Professional Boundaries

Whenever two people coexist, there is an expectation that boundaries will exist in the relationship. Professional boundaries are a framework that protects both the people receiving services and the service providers. Boundaries allow for safe connections between people, a clear understanding of each party's limits and responsibilities, and appropriate differentiation (or mental/emotional separation) between individuals.

In their article about boundaries, Dietz and Thompson noted, "The concern about appropriate boundaries is, at least in part, a concern about the effects of the power differential between client and professional. It is primarily a concern about boundary violations."[22]

Professional boundaries are imperative for effective service. Adhering to guidelines ensures that the customer's needs come first, business is kept separate from personal matters, and the service provider is demonstrating appropriate behavior to the customer through word and deed. Having good intent is not enough if your actions as a service provider violate the professional boundaries set by your company or the boundaries you set for yourself.

---

[21]ProQOL, "Professional Quality of Life Elements Theory and Measure," last modified 2018, http://proqol.org/Home_Page.php.

[22] C. Dietz and D. Thompson, "Rethinking Boundaries: Ethical Dilemmas in the Social Worker-Client Relationship," Journal of Progressive Human Services 15, no. 2 (2004): 1–24, doi:10.1300/J059v15n02•01.

Lisa Jordan, the president of Human Solutions in Buena Park, California, offers principles to consider when establishing and maintaining professional boundaries.[23]

"Empower, Not Rescue"

Advocates are to offer suggestions and give warriors general assistance, "point them in the right directions, nurture the attitude needed, give them encouragement—but don't do the work for them!" America's Warrior Partnership's model is designed to empower, not enable.

"Take Care of Yourself"

Set work boundaries and stick to them. This includes setting work hours, leaving work at work (resist the impulse to answer work calls after hours). Seeking input from coworkers or supervisors about specific troublesome issues can often help you find a new perspective.

"Service Time Is Not 'Me' Time"

Resist the urge to share too much information about yourself. You need to be seen as an advisor, not a friend. "Active listening places the proper focus on your customers' needs. It also creates an environment of trust." It's not about you; it's about the warrior.

"Don't Open Your Wallet"

Some advocates get themselves started down this slippery path by providing minimal amounts of money for everyday items, then move on to more when asked by a customer. Instead of dipping into your pocket, look for additional funding for specific necessary items from available program money, or find community partners who are willing to provide funding when needed.

"Don't Shift from Service Provider to Employer"

Don't hire or use customers to complete personal tasks. You are working for your customer; they should not be working for you. Working with you or your agency may feel more comfortable than working for another organization. As a result, the warrior may not seek better employment opportunities elsewhere.

---

[23]L. Jordan, "8 Principles for Effectively Maintaining Boundaries as a Service Professional," last modified February 24, 2012, https://human-solutions.net/8-principles-for- effectively-maintaining-professional-boundaries-as-a-service-provider/.

"Be Consistent"

Always do what you say you are going to do. Trust is developed through consistency and being true to your word. Resist the urge to overpromise. Additionally, treat all warriors, even the difficult ones, with the same respect and kindness.

"Be a Role Model"

Always be professional in your behavior. This includes your language and word choices as well as punctuality. All warriors should be treated with the respect they have earned by their service. Advocates should be seen as customer service representatives working as an expert in their field for warriors.

"Be Accountable"

As with any job, it is essential for advocates to keep their supervisors updated with information about potential trials or triumphs. Supervisors can often offer great advice and strategies for dealing with tricky situations. Additionally, consider finding a supportive coworker who can provide you with guidance when needed. These support people will be invaluable when circumstances get complicated and will assist you in handling your responsibilities professionally.

CHAPTER 9:
COMMUNITY INTEGRATION MISCONCEPTIONS

What's in this chapter?

✓ Common misconceptions that interfere with the successful implementation of the Community Integration model

✓ Scenarios of common misconceptions in action

✓ An explanation of the problems revealed in the misconception scenarios

"If you do what you've always done, you'll get what you've always gotten."

~ Tony Robbins, Author

Misconception 1: Outreach can be done from your desk.

> *Jenny sips some hot tea while sitting at her newly clean desk, admiring her master's diploma neatly hung on the wall. She looks over her outreach reports from the first six months of initiating Community Integration. She notices that her outreach numbers have continuously declined since month three. Jenny starts to daydream about the possibilities and tries to understand why this is happening: "There are over three thousand veterans within my service area. Outreaching to eight-three veterans per month appears like it would be an easy task, but I cannot seem to outreach to more than twenty-five veterans on average."*
>
> *Jenny then thinks about the efforts she has made to let people know about Community Integration and the services her program offers: "We have notified partners, created email/social media campaigns, and even updated our website to include a self-referral form. What more can we do?"*

Jenny is suffering from a common misconception that she can outreach to veterans from the office. *Outreach*, as it pertains to this program, is often used as a verb, not a noun. The *Merriam-Webster Dictionary* lists the definition of *outreach* as "1: to go too far; 2: to reach out." Outreach, in the Community Integration program, is the act of finding veterans.

If an employee responsible for boots-on-the-ground outreach is getting too comfortable in the office, it is a sign that he or she does not understand outreach. A boots-on-the-ground outreach employee should have a laptop, a cell phone, and a portable printer and should rarely be seen in the office. The employee may not have just one office but instead have hot desks at multiple locations with partnering organizations.

Outreach cannot be done in the office. To repeat, outreach **cannot** be done in the office. This is a critical point to understand when implementing Community Integration. Community Integration is about building relationships; it is connecting with veterans to build trust and understand their individual wants and needs. It is difficult to create relationships when you don't actually meet the veteran in his or her environment. Outreach is about meeting veterans where they are in the community.

Misconception 2: When you have met one, you have met them all.

> *Charles is at a local coffee shop, sitting down with a veteran to perform a formal intake. He is going through the typical questions: Are you employed? Are you enrolled in school? What level of education have you completed? He asks the veteran further details about his employment and education. Charles hears a little bit about the veteran's hourly employment with the local school system as a janitor and hears that the veteran has a bachelor's degree in communications. He tunes out of the remainder of the conversation and starts building a plan for the veteran's employment. He cuts the veteran off midsentence and says, "I would like to update your résumé so that we can work on furthering your career."*
>
> *The veteran looks at Charles, confused, and says, "I like my job." The veteran goes on to explain: "I chose my career as a janitor because I like giving back to my community. As a janitor for the school, I ensure the classrooms are in great shape each evening for the students the next day. It gives me a strong purpose and connection with my community. I am looking for more opportunities to volunteer." Charles is taken aback by the discussion and apologizes for the communication breakdown.*

In this story, Charles is assuming that what one veteran wants is what all veterans want. From his past experiences, he has seen veterans wishing to turn their hourly jobs into salary jobs. He immediately tried to fit this particular veteran into that box. As discussed in the Community Integration principles, one size fits one. This means that what one veteran wants or needs is not necessarily what all veterans want or need. Engagement, as discussed previously in chapter 3, is about knowing the warrior. Community Integration is about understanding a veteran's individual wants and needs. Charles is suffering from unconscious bias in this story, which removes his ability to know the warrior. *Engage*, like *outreach*, is also a verb as it pertains to Community Integration.

If you find yourself "spacing out" during a formal intake, you are not properly engaging with the veteran. An intake is formal in the sense of documentation, but it doesn't have to be formal in its delivery. A formal intake should be about knowing the warrior. You may find that conversation jumps around during a formal intake. This is acceptable and even encouraged. If you have an interest in something the veteran is discussing, ask for further details. If you can find common ground with the veteran, that is even better. Again, Community Integration is about building relationships.

You cannot build a relationship with someone if you are not honestly getting to know him or her. If you cannot put a face with the name in your customer relationship management (CRM) system, then you most likely did not properly engage with the veteran.

Misconception 3: Documentation slows me down and takes the heart out of my job.

> *The program manager and Joanne are sitting down in the office and discussing the internal program audit findings. The program manager confronts Joanne about lack of proper documentation. Joanne pleads her case, saying, "I do not have time to provide documentation because I am trying to build a relationship with veterans to understand their wants and needs. I am too busy to enter data into the CRM. How am I supposed to do a good job with building a relationship while my nose is in a computer?"*
>
> *The program manager listens to Joanne's case and ponders her response. Then the program manager pulls up a veteran contact within the CRM. The program manager asks Joanne, "Can you please tell me the wants and needs of Mr. Smith, whom you met on October first of last year?"*
>
> *Joanne repeats in her head, "Mr. Smith, Mr. Smith . . ." Then she*

> *says, "Can I see the contact information?" The program manager*
> *turns the computer around and shows Joanne the information.*
> *Joanne reads the contact and sees a basic intake of the veteran's status*
> *with employment, education, health care, housing, and benefits.*
> *The contact information does not include an intake plan, does not*
> *describe anything about the veteran's personal interests, and does not*
> *describe the person's marital/family status. Joanne says to the program*
> *manager, "I know Mr. Smith has a full-time job, is not enrolled in*
> *school, has health-care insurance, is permanently housed, and declined*
> *enrollment in benefits."*
>
> *The program manager responds, "Building a relationship isn't just*
> *about knowing a person's current needs; it includes sustaining the*
> *relationship over time. If your documentation is complete and you*
> *know a warrior's interest, you can reach out to the warrior when*
> *opportunities become available that would improve the warrior's*
> *quality of life."*

There is a common misconception among employees, especially ones who want to change the world (aka "do-gooders"), that documentation makes veterans just a number. This case provides you with an example of how documentation could have actually improved Joanne's relationship with the warrior. Documentation is just as important as getting to know the veteran through an attentive conversation. As discussed in misconception 2, the discussion may jump around when building a relationship with the veteran. This is OK and actually encouraged. It is the advocate's job to learn how to balance conversation and documentation. When you build trust with veterans, they may be less uncomfortable waiting for you to jot down a few notes and asking them to repeat details about themselves.

If you encounter employee resistance to documentation, you should emphasize that your CRM is there to help build a relationship. Documentation helps reduce duplication of efforts. If the proper information is documented at the beginning, the veteran is less likely to become frustrated with the same question being asked multiple times.

The misconception that documentation slows you down is a myth; it actually speeds up the process of collaboration and getting veterans the services they need. Additionally, it gives you the information you need to develop relationships that can truly improve the quality of life for warriors.

Misconception 4: When you solve a case, your relationship with the veteran is done.

"Case closed," Sandra says to her coworker. "I am really going to miss this veteran. Her personality was such a breath of fresh air. She was always very eager to learn about resources in the area, had excellent communication skills, and was very proactive." Sandra compiles the veteran's paperwork in a file folder and walks away from her desk toward the secure file room. Sandra continues the conversation with her coworker when she returns to her desk: "I am so glad she found a rewarding job in the field she is interested in. She will do a great job as an office manager for the health-care clinic."

The coworker asks Sandra about the case: "Sandra, what makes you think you will not see this veteran again?"

Sandra stops to think for a moment and says, "I helped her find a job. My services are no longer needed."

The coworker responds, "Does this veteran have all the resources she needs?"

Sandra replies, "I am not sure I understand what you are asking. She came into the office asking for assistance finding a job. I found her a job."

The coworker is trying to get Sandra to think about the Community Integration model. Maintaining a relationship even after services have been received is pivotal. The Community Integration model is about knowing the veteran. You cannot know veterans if you do not stay in touch with them. Community Integration is about celebrating successes, creating opportunities to give back, and being there if issues arise. By staying in touch with veterans and maintaining a strong relationship, you are able to serve them beyond their initial needs. We often find that, once a veteran is helped, he or she wants to pay it forward. You should be there to pick up the call when a veteran has this request. Additionally, when veterans are connected to a resource, they might find they need another resource to further their future and improve their quality of life. As their advocate, you want to be the first one they call to connect to more resources.

Maintaining a relationship is about constantly checking in with veterans and communicating with them. Whether it is asking for a follow-up request three months after the veteran receives services, connecting them to a newsletter, or connecting them to community events that might interest them and their family members, maintaining ways to connect with them is important.

The four-step plan is a continuum of care. Connections should be done regularly even after the veteran has received services. Education creates opportunities for you to connect with veterans. When a new resource becomes available, you have the opportunity to connect with veterans to let them know about it.

Advocating is continuous. Oftentimes, individuals don't understand their full potential if they do not have someone who believes in them. Lastly, collaboration between veterans and the community leads to the success of all. Veterans are assets within the community. Finding ways to use their skills to improve the lives of all within the community is the key to success.

Misconception 5: Serving a veteran is giving them a piece of paper with instructions.

It's 8:29 a.m. on a Monday in October. Jackson is waiting at a local university veteran resource center for his first appointment of the day. He is meeting with a veteran to complete a formal intake and discuss a plan of action. The veteran enters promptly at 8:30 a.m. for the meeting. During the meeting, Jackson and the veteran discuss basic needs, build a relationship by sharing active-duty stories, and speak about wishes and desires. The veteran and Jackson discuss a plan of action based on the veteran's goals. At the end of the meeting, Jackson hands the veteran a piece of paper with the veteran's next steps. The two shake hands and part ways.

One month passes; Thanksgiving is around the corner, and Jackson wants to check in with his veteran contacts before the holiday rush. Jackson calls the veteran whom he met at the university resource center to ask him how he is doing on making progress. The veteran says he has not had any time to connect with the local resources Jackson had provided, but he would soon. Jackson calls again in December to see if there has been any progress, and the veteran says again that he has not had time. Jackson scratches his head and thinks, "Am I doing something wrong? Why is the veteran not being proactive?"

Jackson is suffering from a common misconception that service is giving a veteran a piece of paper with some numbers on it. Providing a veteran with a piece of paper that lists resources, although helpful, is not the complete service package. Some people like to see what their steps are and like to proactively connect with resources when they have the time. Others need a little nudge. Serving veterans is about understanding what gets them to the resource. Lack of veteran engagement should not be a reoccurring barrier to success. If a veteran does not actively reach out to obtain services, it is the employee's purpose to help the veteran reach out. The section "Serving the Warrior" in chapter 3 is about recruiting multiple service providers and employees to keep the veteran on track to success. Community Integration is about proactive service.

If you see in your reports or CRM dashboards that "lack of engagement" is a continued reason that cases are closed, there is something seriously wrong with your service delivery. Handing a veteran a piece of paper and expecting the veteran to act on that is a mistake. It is your responsibility as a service provider to encourage veterans to receive support. You cannot do this forcefully. You have to use the Community Integration principles and the four-step plan to build a relationship and find what motivates that veteran. If a veteran expresses interest in receiving services, he or she wants your help.

Motivating others is difficult, but that is what you are here for. You are their advocate.

Misconception 6: I can do Community Integration all on my own.

> *Grace is running ragged trying to get her work done. She sighs as she glances down at her list of things to do today. She has just finished reviewing one veteran's résumé and needs to email him a copy of her suggested changes. She has a 10:00 a.m. appointment with another veteran to enroll him in the Department of Veterans Affairs (VA) program. There's a veteran who just walked in the door who needs a Department of Housing and Urban Development–Veterans Affairs Supportive Housing (HUD-VASH) evaluation. Also, there is a list of ten veterans she needs to check in with to follow up on the services they received last month. Grace thinks to herself, "How am I going to get all this done today?" Just as she is thinking that her schedule is maxed out, the program manager walks in and tells Grace that there is a community event she needs to attend today at 3:00 p.m. Grace says, "I got it." Grace sits back in her chair and continues to prioritize her activities. She thinks, "The follow-up with the ten veterans can wait until tomorrow, but the remaining, I'm afraid, cannot wait. There needs to be more hours in the day."*

You cannot do Community Integration all on your own. In this case, Grace is starting to realize this. Every community has resources that can improve the quality of life of veterans. It is the Community Integration leader's responsibility to connect with each of the resources available and use them to their full potential. If there is a resource for employment, the Community Integration leader should be focused on finding veterans who need employment and connecting them to the employment partner. Then, once the veteran receives the services he or she needs, it is the responsibility of the Community Integration leader to check back with the veteran and continually engage with the veteran.

Community Integration is about finding veterans, knowing veterans, and connecting them to resources within the community that are already available. You cannot implement Community Integration without understanding this concept. Community Integration is not about reinventing the wheel and becoming the one nonprofit within the community that provides direct services to veterans. Direct services are already covered by other nonprofits within the community. It is difficult to enter a community if you plan to do Community Integration on your own. This may appear threatening to the livelihood of other organizations. Additionally, doing Community Integration all on your own is not sustainable. You will need to raise more funds to provide direct services, and your staff may become exhausted, as you can see in Grace's case. Grace had to put off follow-up because of her busy schedule. Follow-up is a pivotal part of Community Integration. If you find your staff putting off critical principles of Community Integration like follow-up while getting into the weeds of direct services, you are not doing Community Integration as it is intended.

FURTHER ASSISTANCE

America's Warrior Partnership offers support and tools to assist your organization and community with implementing Community Integration.

Our consulting services are designed as a phased approach that tailors the Community Integration program to your context, budget, and strategic growth plan.

America's Warrior Partnership assesses the current state of veteran services in your community, offers options for the speed and size of your program development, brings training and mentorship to your organization, and supports you throughout your implementation process with individual guidance, an annual survey, and an audit. We provide technical assistance in specialized areas ranging from marketing and fundraising to nonprofit operations and program management. Additionally, as new staff members are on-boarded, we provide on-demand training to get them up to speed fast.

Our WarriorServe® information system supports your efforts to develop and maintain relationships with warriors while also connecting your service partners in an efficient case-coordination platform. Dashboards and reports allow you to analyze the effectiveness of referrals for services, keep the most critical cases prioritized, and keep a full-service history readily available for any warrior. The Salesforce platform ensures critical data security, high reliability and access, and robust features available to nonprofit organizations at a low price.

When a program reaches affiliation status, America's Warrior Partnership offers program maintenance through continued training, mentorship, and assessments. We provide updated training modules to ensure your program is aware of industry trends and provide an annual Community Integration training workshop to share best practices followed by an annual Community Integration Symposium to meet with industry leaders and collaborate with national service providers. We offer sustained mentorship through continued access to a community manager and ongoing access to WarriorServe® technical support. Finally, America's Warrior Partnership provides monthly metric reports, an annual audit, and an annual warrior survey to continue assessing the program's ability to serve its warriors.

We would be happy to tell you more about consulting services or WarriorServe® and offer a demo or pricing proposal. Contact us at (706) 434-1708.

CPSIA information can be obtained
at www.ICGtesting.com
Printed in the USA
FFHW011934170819
54371237-60071FF